D1554252

THE $ELLING
OF JEU

By Victor V. Bryditzki

Published by Chick Publications
P.O. Box 662, Chino, CA 91710
Printed in the United States of America

Published by Chick Publications
P.O. Box 662, Chino, CA 91710
Printed in the United States of America

Library of Congress Catalog Card No. 85-00000

ISBN 0-937958-22-0

Second Printing ... 1986

193/B

Dedication

Dedicated in general to those brave Christian Bookstores that originally started out as a ministry and were finally forced to end up as a business in order to survive.

Dedicated more specifically to Fay Palmer and Jan Allgier of the Amazing Grace Bookstore in Grass Valley, California, who were a constant source of encouragement, love, and compassion during our lonely journey through the religious wilderness. These two lovely saints gave in spite of their own terrible wounds that were inflicted also by those they came to serve.

Preface

The Selling of Jeu — The Confessions of a Christian Bookstore Owner is an on-the-spot, behind-the-scenes story of the "Jesus business" told in the first person by someone who survived this "ministry."

Like many other idealistic Christians we always dreamed of someday opening a Christian Bookstore as a meaningful and peaceful way to spend one's golden years, but our dream turned into a nightmare. Caught in a no-win situation, our hopes and our aspirations were finally buried in potter's field, buried by the very ones we came to serve — the visible church.

This true story, written with some sarcasm and a touch of humor takes a very important and serious subject and gives it a smile, but leaves the final conclusion up to the reader. It will unfortunately reveal that the one all-important asset that professing Christians claim to have, love, is the one fruit they are completely destitute of. And if we hate someone that we have seen . . . how can we possibly love Someone that we have not seen?

The story will appeal to all denominations and every position, from publisher, to pulpit, to pew . . . if they have the courage to admit that they are capable of doing such things . . . all in the name of JESUS!

Contents

Victor V. and Dorothy Bryditzki

CHAPTER 1

Valium, Nitro and $108

The courtroom arena was still empty, so I sat down to wait for the lions. A few people came in and sat here and there. Then a "California dressed" man — very slick — entered and called out my name. He said he was the attorney for the JEU Company who had summoned me here. He wanted to know if we could put this all over to another date, since he had forgotten to bring his file with him today. I didn't think I could go through this again; I was well primed with valium and nitroglycerine, and I wanted to get it over with. So I declined a postponement.

"'Scuse me," he said, "but how much money do you owe my client?"

"A hundred and eight dollars," I answered.

"You mean I drove all the way up from Sacramento for a crummy $108?!"

"It's your party," I replied, "you invited me, remember?"

"Listen, why waste a lot of time. Why don't you just agree to a judgment and then I can get out of here?"

"I'm sorry, but you people added all kinds of interest and other charges, which makes your claim $424.00. I can't agree to that."

"I'll tell you what. Why don't you agree right now to pay me in small monthly payments and we'll just forget bothering the judge."

"No. I want to see the judge."

"You don't understand. I've got a real important case to go to . . . "

"I'm sorry, but you served me papers to be here this morning, and I'm here." He paced back and forth like a caged lion, glancing at his watch every other minute, and mumbling under his breath. I could see he was losing patience.

At last a court clerk came out and called my name. He brought us both into the judge's chambers. His honor was in his shirt sleeves. He appeared kind and was soft-spoken. "Good morning, gentlemen. Let's see, what do we have here?" He read over the summons and commented, "Hmmm, there's nothing much here to go to trial on."

He asked me, "Are you contesting this?"

"No, sir," I replied. "Here's a copy of my letter that I sent to the company acknowledging that there are still four invoices unpaid and explaining why I was unable to pay at this time, but promising that I would. We pay by invoice, and their computer keeps spitting out these statements and my balance keeps growing each month to almost three times what I really owe. They're charging interest on top of interest."

"That's impossible," he exclaimed.

"Here, see for yourself." I laid a bunch of statements on his desk.

He shook his head. "I don't believe this, but it's legal. What we have here, then, is that you admit you owe the money, but you are questioning the amount."

"Yes, sir."

"Will you agree to pay your invoices, plus the court costs?"

"I can't today, sir. I don't have the money."

"But will you agree to that amount?"

"Why do I have to pay court costs? I admitted from the beginning that I owed the money. I never contested it or denied it."

"You'll have to take that up with the publisher; they filed the suit. But since the costs are here, someone has to pay them, and you're our Number 1 candidate."

"It doesn't sound too fair."

"Well, it's either that, or we have to go to trial over this ridiculous amount and then there will be even more court costs. It's better for you to quit while you're ahead."

So I agreed.

"How does that sound to you, counselor?"

The lawyer agreed.

"Fine. It's settled. I'll have the necessary papers drawn up. Thank you, gentlemen."

As I walked out, I couldn't help wondering what the judge really thought. He had been fair and honest, showing more kindness and understanding than the JEU Company. I wondered if he was a Christian? Did he know about I Cor 6:1-8 — how Christians are supposed to act in such a situation? How embarrassing!

On the way home, I stopped at the bank. I shouldn't have. From embarrassment I was promoted to humiliation. At the window I learned that the sheriff was in that morning to withdraw $108.05 from my checking account to satisfy a small-claim court judgment filed by a JEU junk dealer in Southern California — and this amount, mind you, was for **interest** on a **paid** invoice! And that was the good news! The bad news was that this withdrawal depleted our account so that checks written were bouncing like tennis balls under a racket. What a "racket" this JEU business is!

The handwriting had been on the proverbial wall for some time; we should have bailed out a long time ago. But all we had ever wanted was to provide our town a Christian bookstore that would be a real help — a ministry and business combined. We kept hoping that God could still use us and would somehow restore our financial stability. The time was past for godly planning; nothing short of a miracle would do now.

Our home was already on the market. That's not big news, many people sell their homes to rescue their finances; it's becoming a common experience. What is not common is to have the title company tell you in front of agents and other people that there is a lien against your property — filed by a West coast "Christian" book distributor.

"But I paid that bill," I exclaimed in mortification.

"You may have, but apparently you still owe $41 in interest, plus the court costs for filing this lien!"

I drove home thinking, this can't be happening; I'm having a nightmare. Soon, very soon, I hope, I'll wake up in my own bed surrounded by loving pagans, giving heathens, nonjudgmental atheists, forgiving agnostics, and live-and-let-live skeptics — the

13

regular, normal people of this world that I once knew and loved, the ones who loved me and even said "Thank you" when I did them a favor. Maybe everything is just upside down? That's it! Maybe the unsaved are the Christians and the "Christians" are unsaved; we've just got our terms mixed up. Like the despised dog-bone Samaritan and the holy Pharisees, things are turned around.

Battered and forlorn, I drove into my own driveway thinking I would get a respite from the battlefield. But my wife met me at the door to urge me to make haste; she was with a young girl that she felt was beyond her ability to help.

I recognized Mary immediately; she had been in the store many times. For her 24 years, she had been through a lot, but always had a smile. Today she didn't.

For the next hour, I listened, counseled, taught, encouraged, and prayed for Mary. She was guilt-ridden, spiritually frustrated, in despair, feeling deserted by God and no help in sight. Her regular "pastor" had worsened her state of despair, feeling this was the time to reprimand her for wearing lipstick, for being too "worldly," and not living up to her church commitment.

"I can't be what 'they' want me to be," she exclaimed. "When I act like they want me to, I feel like a phony. But I'm scared that God will punish me, and I don't want to go to hell." She was sobbing now. "I'm just not perfect like they tell me I should be. I guess I'm not a Christian like I thought I was . . . but I really don't want to fail God. I'm scared. Please help me."

My teaching consisted of explaining terms that she apparently had never heard before. Carefully, I explained the terms substitute, propitiation, atonement, imputation, justification, Mediator. These are not idle

14

terms — they mean something. If we flawed human beings have to reach a state of sinless perfection before we can gain heaven — then who is going to get there? Further, we have robbed the Christ event of its meaning — if we are going to gain heaven by our own efforts, then we need no substitution, imputation, justification, or mediation. When Mary was able to take her eyes off herself and fastened them onto her Saviour, the Second or Last Adam (whose righteousness was sufficient for the many even as Adam's sin had contaminated the many, I Cor 15: 21-22), she was able to forget her human failings and she cried tears of relief.

After we had prayed together, she asked, "Is this why my Pastor calls you 'dangerous,' because you use such big words?"

"Well . . . I don't think so. You see, the words aren't really big at all. They just describe a big work, the sufficient work of a big, Almighty and Sovereign God. Some people just can't accept this idea of such a big God; they are more comfortable with a smaller god they can control. They don't realize they are creating a worse problem for themselves when they reduce the size of their god. They obscure the work of Christ on the cross and take the main work of salvation on their own shoulders — which is an impossible task. Until we come face to face with the big God of the Bible, we are just living a fool's paradise. And that **is** phony — you were right to recognize the phoniness of such self-deception. But people are always fearful of whatever threatens the small worlds they made for themselves."

"I was told not to talk to you, but I'm glad I did!" Mary's face showed relief and joy.

"I'm glad you did, too, Mary. I really needed to share the God of the Bible with someone today, and

15

apparently God chose you. Thank you!"

It was true that on this day I needed Mary even more than she needed me. The lions may growl, but my Saviour triumphed over all, even shame and embarrassment.

But let's go back and see how this victory came in the middle of despair.

CHAPTER 2

In the Beginning . . .

People say it's impossible, but I can actually remember being in a wicker baby carriage and crying to get my mother's attention while she was playing tennis. My memory bank even goes back to my first steps in the kitchen of our upper Fell Street flat in San Francisco and learning to walk. I especially remember how frightened I was when my father carried me to the altar to receive communion from a long-bearded priest dressed in strange gold attire. His deep vibrating basso chants scared the be-jeebers out of me — it was like facing God!

As a child I spoke only Russian. My parents were immigrants who came to America after the 1917 Revolution. My father was an officer in the Czar's army, but the Bolsheviks won in spite of that fact, and he was wise enough to leave Russia while he could, even though it meant great material loss to him. My mother also came from royalty, and my earliest memories recall her dispensing royal hospitality, a habit she never lost.

We moved when I was three so I could grow up in a better neighborhood. Since I spoke only Russian, the kids on the block in the "better neighborhood" used to beat me up and throw rocks at me. My only friend was a little Jewish kid who used to get beat up too. Since we had something in common, we became friends.

In kindergarten I became bilingual, of course. But to make sure I did not lose my Russian heritage, my mother sent me twice a week to Russian school after I got out of public school. I also had piano lessons twice a week from Madam Boris. She was a real "Boris" too! She cracked me over the knuckles with her stick each time I played a wrong note. Saturdays were for "Sunday School," or religious training at our Russian Orthodox Church and Sundays were Church itself. Services lasted for hours and we all stood. Sitting was only for old women and cripples. I used to look at them and think they were lucky.

Our home was always filled with people singing, laughing, eating, drinking (tea or vodka), and reminiscing over the "good old days" before the Bolsheviks came. There were also endless numbers of religious celebrations and our 12-foot dining room table was always covered with delicacies from another life. I loved it!

By high-school age, I was living in two distinct worlds: one with my beloved parents, the other the new and exciting world of America. Then teenage rebellion set in with all its ramifications. Once, against my parents' wishes, I played in a musical combo for an Italian wedding reception that was held in the "wrong" district (for me). During intermissions the "Italiano" buffet table was at our disposal, including drinks. When the leader of the group paid me 25 dollars for playing the piano, I couldn't believe it. That was a fortune back in those days. I felt I was a millionaire!

No one told me I wasn't qualified to organize a band of my own so I did just that. Because I was raised on Tschaikowsky, Rimsky-Korsakov and Rachmaninoff, I just didn't have "rhythm" so I bought, borrowed and stole every swing record I could get my hands on. I played them until I had memorized every note. I made a total musical blood transfusion into this wonderful thing called "jazz." My parents, of course, were horrified. For my band I wanted the best musicians I could find, so I went looking everywhere for them. In some places I heard, "Hey white boy, whatcha doin' down here?" Then when I got back to my "better" neighborhood we heard, "Hey, what's that nigger doin' here?" My reply was, "It's cool man, he's with me." It was enough to pacify the invisible gang borderlines. (My Americanization, apparently, was complete!)

The fruit of my faithful searches was the best "teenage" band in the city. We were Miller, Dorsey, Goodman and Kenton all rolled into one. We played dances, shows, clubs, downtown theaters, and even radio. During the 40's the liquor laws for minors were lax, so my piano was always crowded with free drinks from patrons and my tolerance for alcohol was incredible.

When I was 19 I was disowned by my parents. At 20 I entered the military. The Korean War was in full "police action" but since I was a native-born

American, fluent in Russian, I was placed in Military Intelligence. (My mother's insistence on Russian training had saved me from dying in the rice fields in Asia). Stationed on the Iron Curtain in Europe, with full security clearance, I was a translator-interpreter for the 7th Army. I interrogated prisoners, translated captured documents, and interpreted diplomatic conversations. We lived in German villas, wore civilian clothes, and drank ourselves to oblivion.

Life on the border between East and West was tense, like a bomb ready to explode. So I began reading my Bible — for insurance — just in case. It must have worked because I came home alive. Home again, I learned that too many of my musician friends had been killed in Korea. That decided me against a return to music. I was feeling bitter and wanted to begin a whole new life.

Through a friend, I got a job with one of the biggest furniture companies in the city, and I started climbing the proverbial American business ladder toward material success. When I could climb no higher where I was, I went elsewhere for bigger and better opportunities. After several years of work, I had my own decorating store. Everything I touched seemed to turn to gold (although it involved working 7 days and 6 nights a week). But the more money I made, the more I spent. My bar bill was astronomical.

Somewhere in this whirlwind life style, I met one lovely lady. We fell in love and flew off to Reno. Our marriage was heaven-on-earth and a battlefield at the same time. When we weren't loving each other we were killing each other. One of our many problems was that she was divorced (with two children) and this made our marriage illegal in the eyes of her Catholic religion. The two additional children from our union were considered illegitimate and she was given the typical Catholic curse. Other people cannot fathom what a mental, spiritual, and psychological trauma this is. There's only one thing worse, and that is to live with someone who has been cursed by the Catholics. It was terrible!

A form of temporary relief was given us when some Jehovah's Witnesses convinced my wife that the Catholics were wrong and that she was not going to a place called Hell. But the peace was short-lived. The more they taught, the more a new problem protruded its ugly head into our marriage. Now we had a religious war, and no feelings were spared. My wife clung to her only hope of sanity and I became a man obsessed to prove the Jehovah's Witnesses to be wrong in their teachings.

At that time I did not know that a Christian bookstore existed. I never had a need for one. Concordances, Topical Bibles, reference books, were non-existent to me. All I had was an old King James Bible, and I began tearing into it. My childhood memories told me that between the covers of this black book was proof that the new and strange doctrines of the Witnesses were all wrong. I read and read, night after night, until 2 or 3 o'clock in the morning. I put my Bible under my pillow hoping that information would somehow pass into my brain by osmosis. I was a man possessed! I even read while driving to and from work. Weeks turned into months and even years. I found my proof, I was convinced . . . but nobody was listening. The Words of God fell on deaf ears.

CHAPTER 3

God's Great Mercy

Some Christians do not remember exactly when they were saved. I'm sure the most important thing is the knowledge that one **is** saved and when it happened is unimportant by comparison. But my own case was so dramatic that I know the day, the hour, and even the spot where God gave me a new birth. My entrance into the Kingdom was quite different than usual . . . and perhaps this difference explains the passion that I still have for God, His Word, and His Truth.

Before salvation, my wife and I were not involved with any church, we were not tutored on how to become a Christian by "accepting Jesus into your hearts" or "going forward," or any of the usual ways one hears in today's churchianity. Up to that day, it was only the written Word of God and me. I was as ignorant of the "decision" methods as I was of God's sovereign grace. The Bible to me was only a means of proving to someone else what I already knew to be true. Little did I know that by spending so much time in the Scriptures the living and transforming Word was being infused into my soul where the Holy Spirit could use it to bring light into darkness.

One Sunday afternoon we were spending the weekend as we often did in our country home in the Santa Cruz mountains. In spite of the heavenly setting, my wife and I were at it again, continuing our bitter, never-ending fight. (How weary it was . . . living with imperfection!) We started home in two cars, my wife and our children in one, I in the other.

My emotions were devastated. I could see that my marriage along with my whole life was a failure, and changing it was a hopeless task. The continual bickering and constant open fighting between us had brought me to the point of despair. I even considered driving my car off the coast highway to crash on the rocks below — but I was afraid I might hurt myself. In the privacy of my car I shouted every obscenity I could think of, mostly directed at my wife, who I felt was the cause of all my misery. And my misery was now so great that I could bear it no longer.

I was in a double-bind. I couldn't stand to live, and I wasn't brave enough to die. I knew my situation was hopeless on the human level. I cried out to God, not for salvation for I didn't know I needed it, but for relief, for escape from **myself;** from the terrible person I knew myself to be. As I drove past Beanhollow Beach, I was deeply engrossed in pleading with God. "Change me or kill me," I cried repeatedly. I also prayed out loud in Russian just in case God would have more compassion and pity on a Russian soul. I found myself, somewhat hysterically, begging God to forgive me for being what I was. I was crying so much by this time I could not even see the road. When I reached the top of the hill, I was reduced to just sobbing quietly. Turning my bloodshot eyes to the West, I noticed the sun just going down into the Pacific Ocean. Little did I know that my old life, my old self and my sins, were being buried in the sea with that very sunset.

By the time I reached home I was exhausted. I went to bed early. The following week was "weird" or "different," without my being able to say why. I was a split personality. I worried I was really going off the deep end. Saturday evening we were involved in one of our many cocktail parties. My wife and I were also at it again, giving me the legal excuse to drink with both hands. I was so angry at her I wanted to smoke myself to death . . . nicotine suicide! But the more I smoked, the worse they tasted. I tried OP's (other people's) but they tasted even worse than my own. How disgusting! I couldn't even die with a pleasant taste in my mouth. I simply could not smoke no matter how hard I tried.

Several of our guests began to request one of my speciality "talents." I was an excellent teller of "off-color" jokes. I had every accent down pat but of course my best was my "Roosky" accent. But for some strange reason, this stand-up comedian could not remember a single line. My store of jokes numbered in the hundreds, and I had always been able to recite, any or all, at the most feeble request. Now I could not remember even one! My mental computer had a complete breakdown! What was happening to me? Was senility setting in before its time?

At work I was developing another strange

symptom. Every time someone swore using God's name in vain, I felt a sharp pain in my chest as if stabbed with a spear. The typical four-letter gutter words seemed to have departed from my vocabulary as if I had never learned them. My friends thought I was going nuts. I was inclined to agree with them.

The things that had been natural for me to do, I could no longer do. I recall that I felt a terrible regret for the wrong things I had done, and things that were previously uncomfortable for me, suddenly seemed like a natural thing to do. When I began talking about Jesus everyone ran in different directions.

What was happening? I wondered if I had religion of the brain . . . a very terrible disease . . . I understood! One of my customers was a Baptist minister, and I thought perhaps he would be the right physician for my illness, being a "man of the cloth" and all. So I went to him and told him my story in detail. I thought I had gone "one step beyond" and was being victimized by forces "from the other side" but as I confessed my "spacy" symptoms, he jumped up and went leaping around the room praising God. "And I thought I was bad off," I thought to myself, "this fellow is really wacko!"

"Don't you know what has happened to you?" he asked excitedly.

"If I did, I wouldn't be asking you," I replied.

"You're saved. You've been born again!"

"I'm what?"

"Born again! Here, let me read this passage to you from John, Chapter 3."

I was familiar with the passage but must confess I didn't know what it meant. When he explained it to me I fell back in my chair and wept. I was speechless and awestruck. He prayed for me and as I started to leave he shook my hand violently like I was a long-lost relative. (Little did I know that I was.) He was grinning from ear to ear. Boy, he sure is friendly for being just a casual acquaintance, I was thinking . . .

On my way home, I noticed something I had never seen before: "Calvary Bible Book Store." Now I had driven down this street a thousand times before and I had never noticed this place. I immediately stopped the car and parked right in front. I walked in and told the lady I was a newborn Christian and asked her what I should read. She loaded me with an armful of books. Trusting her selections, I went home to begin reading the first books in my new library.

CHAPTER 4

Booby Traps

A short time later, God reached down from heaven and touched my wife with His grace and saved her. Taken from darkness into light, she dismissed the Jehovah's Witnesses from our home. The Bible alone was more than sufficient; we had no need of human (mis) interpreters. But to this day my wife has a warm spot in her heart for those very kind but very misled people. They were the human instrument that God used to change our lives around. If it wasn't for that knock on the door, we could still be sitting in blind "happiness" in the City of Destruction.

Now we were both in a period of transition. We were shedding our old ways and putting on new. It was much too early for hallelujahs, and our progress was not always simultaneous or even balanced. For example, my wife could not drink any more, but she still smoked. My problem was the other way around. There we were, going at it again, me with a drink in my hand and she with a burning cigarette stuck to her fingers, shaking our fists at one another and shouting in unison, "And you call yourself a Christian! Ha! You're nothing but a hypocrite!" Oh, we were far from perfect, but we knew we were forgiven. Now all we had to learn was to forgive each other.

Someone has said that the best part of fighting is making up, and we had ample opportunity to prove the truth of that remark. It was a lot of fun making up. But more important is this Biblical truth: a forgiven person is someone who is progressively more and more forgiving himself. One who has been forgiven much is now able to love much. Those who are touched by grace live in a realm of inner tenderness, conscious of the grace tendered to them. Those who are truly at peace with God are at peace with one another. This canopy finally settled over our home. Peace at last.

Being church-oriented from our youth, we shortly joined our local "nondenominational-Bible-believing-community church." This was in fact our local "spirit-filled — charismatic — assembly" and our exciting visible-church life went into full swing. We were active-active church members. We attended both Sunday morning and evening services, prayer meetings, potlucks, seminars, every special meeting, and had Bible studies in our home. Our church was our home and our home was our church; our kids were going to "believe" even if they didn't.

Now we started a cycle some of you will recognize. We were told to "die to self" and "live to the Lord." We did our best. To show our love to God, we were encouraged to "give" and give we did: money, time, material possessions. It was obvious to us that God needed us. He needed our money and our earthly acquirements. Whatever God needed, if we had it, we gave it. He could have it for the asking — and there was lots of asking. The church kept asking and we kept giving. Why not?

Our home happened to be elegant, and it was available to our church. It became the official stopover for every traveling evangelist coming through town. We entertained, dined, and accommodated the best of them. Some of the people who spent time in our home went on to become big spiritual superstars of today. But when we knew them, they were "humble servants of the Lord."

Because I was self-employed, my time was my own, so a lot of time was spent with our pastor and his fellow ministers. God seemed to give them a constant stream of messages. Although I couldn't hear these messages myself, I got the full benefit of them nonetheless. We were always going somewhere, paid for by the church. Once, by the "leading of the Holy Spirit," we went to Mexico to "minister," even though none of us spoke Spanish. But my high-school Spanish actually saved us a few times when we got lost on back roads. We didn't "save" anybody, but we had a lot of fun.

Another time we were "led" to drive to Los Angeles on a "special mission" of the Lord, but somehow the Spirit detoured us to go shopping in Tiajuana. When my pastor was "led" to minister to the lost in New Zealand, I was disappointed that the Holy Spirit didn't tell him to take me along. Especially when the Spirit told him to take a short-cut home through Europe. Even in spite of such setbacks, it was fun living among the gods — the "anointed ones" of the visible church.

31

It was suggested that we should sell our home and give the money to God. The idea was to send it on ahead to heaven, making sure of our reservations at the heavenly banquet facilities. Being obedient, God-loving and fearing, and utterly stupid, we put our home on the market. But by the time the house sold, we had a falling out between ourselves and the church, so God got cheated out of the money we planned to send "on ahead." Instead we became "missionaries" and went to work in a "Christian" (how dumb can you get?) camp in the mountains. At first it was great fun, but as soon as the novelty wore off, we saw that our first real "ministry" was actually a total disaster. It was terrible.

Beware of those "vows of poverty" other people are always trying to push onto you. Mostly they are for those who never had anything in the first place, and don't know how to get it in the second place. We learned fast what it is like to live and work with professing "Christians" intent on self-emulation. Stay home, young man, stay home!

Lots of people have had early experiences like ours. The wonder is that some survive to become Christians who love God and truth. The bad part is that there are so many booby traps along the way to plain, earthly Christian living.

CHAPTER 5

Water Turned to Wine

At this time we found ourselves in a remote area of the Santa Cruz mountains. I was "up a tree" without even a leaf to hide my embarrassment or failure. We had burned our bridges behind us, so there was no retreat. Nor could I holler "charge" for I truly didn't know which way to go.

Fortunately for my sanity and for our marriage, we didn't have to stay in this uncertain condition long. The phone rang, and by some fluke, miracle, accident, mistake — or an act of God — I was given a prestigious position as a counselor-instructor at a local penal detention camp for inner city children run by the City and County of San Francisco. This isolated mountain institution housed the city's social

rejects. Most of them were "Zulu basketball players" who made my white six-foot frame appear stunted. I was the only one on the staff who did not have worldly "letters" of achievement after his name. All I had was "B.A. and S.B.G." (born again and saved by grace). Nonetheless, my letters gave me an important and supernatural advantage. I was the only instructor whose classes were void of violence, bloodletting, or (believe it or not) even bad language. The "lettered in psychology" professors were infested with bedlam — continuous verbal and physical conflicts. God put an invisible cover of peace over me and protected me from the verbal attacks and sudden physical assaults on teachers that were common to the reformatory.

In this strange place, I was able to practice what I knew (so far) real Christianity to be. There I began to learn the truth of the saying, "If you're going to preach grace, show grace." When I'm in a philosophical mood I may add, "Those who do not show grace to others, in all probability have never really experienced God's grace themselves."

I cannot say there were no trials involved with this job. Lots of days were touch-and-go, and lots of nights were spent in prayer for one or another of those boys who had lived rough lives and were still a rough lot. Yet God works in mysterious ways. While we were enjoying the economic "blessing" of this job, a man came into my life truly sent of God.

This man was looking for a student, and I was searching for a teacher. Too eagerly, I showed him my large and growing library of current Christian books, the ones I had read so far. I was expecting him to be impressed, perhaps even give me a compliment or a least a smile of approval of my industrious pursuit of Christian reading. Instead, I received a look of disappointment. "If you're going to spend time reading, read **good** books! Get rid of this trash!"

He brought over and literally gave me as a free gift his personal theological library. "Here, if you're going to learn, study the best." With this unheard-of gift, I began my journey into the past. I walked with the greats of Christian literature. This mentor of great Christian reading became not only my spiritual father, but a very close and dear friend to this day. At this time he became my personal and full-time tutor. There, in the quiet of God's forest, we discussed the Scriptures and studied them with insights provided by Gill, Hodge, Spurgeon, Lange, Strong, Pink, Lloyd-Jones, and others of the kind. In the stillness of the towering redwoods, we prayed together that the Holy Spirit would reveal to me the real truths of the Bible.

There is nothing like the silence of giant trees to make God's Word sound loud and clear, echoing through the canyons of time ornamented with cool green ferns. Hearing a great truth and meditating on it while looking up into a vast, star-studded sky, un-dimmed by city lights, is an awesome experience. The absence of people talk, noisy church meetings, and the empty sound of spiritual superstars is a great advantage to learning. To this day, my advice to new Christians if they ask, "Where should we go? What should we do? Which Church? Which Bible study?" is to answer, "Go home! In the quiet of your closet, read the Scriptures for yourself. Pray. Meditate on the Word. If the Holy Spirit can't teach you, no one can. Don't come out of your private 'room' for at least a year!" Paul was alone in the desert for three years before he came out and began associating with the other apostles.

After nearly two intense years of Bible study, circumstances brought my personalized schooling to a close. But before my friend and teacher left the area, he brought me before the Bay Area Presbytery of about 50 ministers of many different denominations, and with the laying on of hands and a very intimate ceremony, I was ordained a minister of the Gospel of Jesus Christ. The seriousness of the event and the wondrous way it came about still hovers over my soul.

How strangely events and circumstances move us about here on earth. I was given a little country church to pastor, but after a year we were unexpectedly moved into the foothills of the Sierra mountains to assist in a prominent "ministry" that needed our background from the boys' camp. There we received the rude awakening of corruption within the "visible church." After a terrible year, we were able to escape the confines of this so-called "Christian" institution and find our freedom again in a neighboring community. We were shaken, but not downed.

A friend of mine wrote a book on "Christian Psychiatry," and he included this very interesting thought: "In the light of such evidence, must we conclude that Christianity is a failure? No! On the contrary, for how can anything be judged a failure when it **hasn't yet been tried?**" When I see or experience failure in Christian circles, I ponder over Larry Jordan's remark.

CHAPTER 6

The Grand Opening

When we unexpectedly came into funds so we could open our Christian bookstore, we were ecstatic. We felt the Lord had provided them, and thanked Him accordingly. Learning of our good fortune, many well-meaning friends advised me to invest this money wisely — in real estate, T-bills, a hamburger franchise, anything but what we were planning to do. "You'll never make any money," they predicted. They were right, but we felt the Lord had provided the money, and we wanted to put it back in "the Lord's work." We are not greedy by nature, and were not looking for a huge, profit-making machine.

Others in town warned us we would never make it; three other bookstores had tried in the past and all failed. I reasoned that their failure was for some other reason — poor location, lack of parking, insufficient inventory, not enough capital — so I ignored the warnings. I was told the local churches would not support us. "Nonsense," I said, "we're nice people!"

We started the store as a family project. We rented a building in what we felt was a good location, with parking, good exposure and a super-plush carpet. We added pecky-cedar walls and shingle accents. It was quite a showplace. We built the islands, racks and shelves, and arranged our newly purchased books according to subject. We added a soft stereo system and heavenly Christian music flowed into every corner. Our balance at the bank sent publishers and distributors hurriedly shipping us tons of cases of books. Everybody wanted part of the action. The UPS delivery men were exhausted from carrying in the heavy cases.

People came in and sat down in amazement. It was truly beautiful. Some even laid down on our soft carpet while examining a book from our vast selections. Some didn't even want to leave at closing time. "It's so peaceful here. I feel like I'm 'home.'" From the way they acted, you would think we were the grandest thing to hit town since gold was discovered a century ago.

We were confident. We felt we had the Lord's blessing, and our town was a growing community. The nearest Christian bookstore was thirty miles away. We were sure that with all our advantages — size, large inventory, location, parking facilities, store arrangement, plus our sincere desire to serve our brethren — our business was our ministry and we would succeed. We didn't plan on or care about making a financial killing. We assumed the store would pay for itself, make us a living, and be a blessing to others. We were **wrong!**

The prophets who told us the town would not support a non-denominational bookstore were right. But we found it was not location, parking, size or inventory that made the difference. We were doing all right — at first. Then, one by one, for one reason or another, churches began to boycott us. Was it the town? Was it me? Was it the churches?

A Bible bookstore sits at the crossroads of several denominations, and our concept of Christianity was in for some rude shocks.

42

CHAPTER 7

Invitations Galore

In the beginning, we were personally invited to
attend every church service in town. We were invited
to potlucks, socials, and even given personal invitations for dinner with the pastors. Being outgoing and
sociable, we reciprocated with dinner invitations of
our own. At first, I thought their invitations were because we were charming, likeable people, easy to
talk to and full of fun. But I soon came to realize that
each church wanted to claim the bookstore for its
own. It was important to them that we become members of their particular group. This I could
understand, and I accepted it with a smile. What
brought a frown across my soul was that I had nothing
in common with the preachers in town. It seemed that

we spoke two different languages. We were neither united in spirit nor of one mind.

There was one older pastor I could relate to. He preached a good Scriptural message, covering the whole counsel of God, "withholding nothing" from his congregation. We found his sermons meaty and his personal conversations meaningful. We felt a bond between us; he spoke and acted like a true brother. But suddenly there was a problem in the church, and he left the area. I was alone.

Some of the pastors felt threatened because I was an ordained minister. Their big question was, "Would I start my own church?" Unwittingly, we stepped on even more toes when we began to minister over the counter at the store. People asked for help, and we thought it was OK for Christians to minister to one another.

People came in with all kinds of personal and/or spiritual problems and Scriptural questions. It soon was obvious that my answers and statements were different than their pastor's. Some came in specifically for counseling. Always, my advice was based on the Scriptures. But again it contradicted what they had already heard from their advisors.

Not wanting conflict with the pastors, I urged people to listen to their own pastors, but no, they wanted to know what I would say. Perhaps they considered me an authority because I owned the bookstore. But the contradictions between myself and many local pastors got back to them and severed whatever tenuous relationships remained between us. I could not deny what I knew to be true in the Scriptures, but I was soon branded "dangerous" with "heretical teachings." Even so, our counseling ministry grew beyond our capabilities for handling it.

Our sales counter was all too often wet with the

tears of pathetic and troubled individuals who sought refuge, solace, and sound Biblical counsel at our store. Either they did not wish to confess their problem to someone they knew too well, like their pastor or fellow parishioners, or they wanted answers that really satisfied their souls.

If my "advice" and counsel came from my own thoughts or those of some small sect or denomination, I might see where I was a threat, but since my reading and study was composed exclusively from authors that have always been acknowledged as comprising mainstream Christianity and biblically sound, I could not understand the "threat."

Our sales counter was also our prayer altar, where we openly prayed for and with people we hardly knew. We lay awake at night wondering, worrying, and deeply troubled by some of the problems confessed to us. In the quiet of midnight we continued to pray for those souls who had confided so much to us. We were equally disturbed to recall the terrible advice they had previously been given by their "spiritual masters."

By this time, I was considered a "sheep stealer" by some envious pastors. Yet the only "meadow" I had to offer was the Word of God. Further, we got to see more of what is going on in what is loosely called "Christian circles" than we wanted to see. The fads of the day combined with lack of true Bible knowledge has wrought some terrible things among the innocents.

A typical example was a pathetic woman who came in to tell us in sobs that her husband was convinced by his "shepherd" that he should spend all his time building a home for the "chief-shepherd-pastor," leaving his wife to tend to their large ranch by herself. She was exhausted, and her savings were steadily depleted to buy materials for the double-digit mansion under construction. Since her "shepherd" had the final say in all matters of life, she had no voice. She felt betrayed, frustrated, and totally disillusioned with "Christianity."

The best we could do was try to point her toward true Christianity. The crowning touch of this sad tale is that, after the luxury house was completed for the "shepherd," there was a sex scandal involving "shep" and another woman. He naturally left the area and the movement, but he took with him all the proceeds from the home that was in his name, free and clear!

Well, it didn't take long for people in town to know where we stood on the moral and spiritual wrongs that existed. There are some things you just cannot keep still about! But it wasn't good for business.

CHAPTER 8

A Dream Turns into a Nightmare

Our lovely dream of owning a Christian bookstore turned into a living nightmare. We woke up to the fact that our definition of "Christian" was not the same definition that others, from publisher to public, seemed to hold. We were caught in a no-win situation.

The first group to become upset with us was the one who wanted statues of madonnas, rosary beads, and deluxe framed pictures of the current pope with votive candles. I have never considered such things Christian, so I never bought any nor intended to. Another group was upset because we carried books by Calvin, Luther, Hodge, Gill — weren't they heretics? They write such terrible things! How could a loving Christian bookstore carry such awful books?

48

Another group demanded to know why books by their denomination were not on our shelves. I never thought of them as a denomination but as a cult, or a sect at best. I didn't want anything I considered outright anti-Biblical in the store. After all, this store was in honor of the Lord Jesus Christ and Him crucified, buried, and resurrected again on the third day for the atonement, justification, and glorification of God's elect. Yet others were upset because we had books on what is called the Reformed faith and the Amillenial position. So we were criticized and chastised for what we didn't carry and for what we did carry.

We found ourselves in the biggest communication gap possible. We were labeled narrow, bigoted, and even "dangerous" because we tried to use the Holy Bible as our guideline. We could not understand the visible church's view of Christianity and they could not understand ours. Let me add that we were not representing any one denomination in our store offerings; we carried books by writers from almost every Protestant denomination. The ones we excluded were those we felt were contradicting the Sacred Text; the Bible had to be our guideline.

We also quickly fell out of grace with several publishers because we shipped back some cases of books. These books were no more Christian than Elmer Gantry. The publisher's attitude was, what do you care if it's Scriptural or not — it sells! Don't you want to make a profit and stay in business?

We wanted to stay in business, all right, but our consciences would not let us keep certain "questionable" titles on our shelves. What the publishers refused to take back in this category we took home and burned in our fireplace. That may seem extreme to some, but we are told that each man must work out his own salvation for himself. For us, we could not pass off this junk as Christian to anybody. That left us no choice except to burn it.

Burning money is not exactly my favorite pastime, so I would mutter a lot. My wife would remind me that her preference had been to open a delicatessen. That way we could be eating up our losses. "But, no, you wanted to open a Christian bookstore! Is the fire warm enough for you, dear?"

All kidding aside, I'm wondering how big that bonfire is going to be when God burns up all the false works of the twentieth century?

CHAPTER 9

In It for the Buck

A minister from one of the evangelical denominations came into the store one day and tactfully insinuated that we were apparently not Christians as we claimed. He said we were in the Christian bookstore business strictly "for the buck" and no other reason.

Taken aback, I prodded for the source of his opinions. His thinking was based on a report from some of his people that we carried books on Mormonism, the Watchtower, Armstrongism, Unity, Christian Science, and so forth. It was apparent to him that we were covering all bases to make sure we didn't miss a sale. As a "Watchman," he felt it was his duty to warn his sheep against our store. But, being big about it, he wanted to give me a chance to confess and repent before I was excommunicated.

I was confused as to what exactly he wanted me to do. I knew what I wanted to do, but I knew I shouldn't do it. Switching to plan "B," I took him by the arm and swiftly marched him over to where the books he referred to sat on the shelf. Caught red-handed! There they were: "Maze of Mormonism . . . The Teachings of Christian Science . . . Counterfeits at Your Door . . . Chaos of the Cults . . . Exposé of Jehovah's Witnesses . . . Heresies Exposed . . . Kingdom of the Cults," etc. Stapled on the shelf was a big sign identifying the section as "Religions in Error."

I'm afraid I was a bit sarcastic. "Should I make the sign bigger, or are the words too difficult for you?"

"Well, I'm not convinced you should be carrying stuff like this."

"Are you familiar with these authors?" I asked.

"No."

"Do you read?"

"Of course I read!" He was nettled. "I read all our official publications."

"Your **official** publications?"

"Yes, from our own convention . . . "

"Look, brother," I interrupted, "I'm sure you feel out of place in a nondenominational bookstore. May I just say this to you before you leave. Next time you send someone in, please have them ask for me. I'll be very happy to explain to them any and every book we have. I don't want them leaving under the wrong impression or doubting our Christianity. If I were in something 'for the buck,' as you put it, it certainly would not be a Christian bookstore! You just don't know who and what we have to put up with."

"Oh, really? It looks like such an easy job," he observed.

"You don't know how hard it can be," I sighed.

He walked out the door and I returned to our sales counter. My wife asked sweetly, "Another well-read minister, dear?"

CHAPTER 10

Our First and Last Jesus Concert

The minister of evangelism in one of the more active churches in our town convinced me that I should help sponsor an upcoming Christian concert. Featured was a nationally known Christian rock group, and the idea was to help this church in their "outreach to the unsaved."

Who could turn down an opportunity to show a willing spirit of cooperation like this? My wife. She was dead set against it, but she was too diplomatic to overrule my head-of-the-house decision.

All we had to do was put up posters in our windows announcing the event and pass out free tickets. This seemed easy enough, but it also indicated our approval of this program. I had given our commitment, so we put up the posters and passed out tickets, talked up the musical, and encouraged customers and their friends to attend.

The evening arrived, and I was happy to see the auditorium jam-packed (minus my wife) which we helped to fill. The stage was loaded with sound equipment; amplifiers and giant speakers were stacked on top of one another. In my old musician days, we had only one mike and that was for the vocalist. We had used pillows to muffle the sound of the drums, but here microphones stood like trees in a forest and there were even two mikes for the drums! I wondered if he was planning to use wet noodles for drumsticks.

The group came out: long hair, torn blue jeans, old T-shirts, leather jackets, and whatever. I couldn't help recalling our old band when we all wore matching blue sports coats, with yellow knit ties over white shirts. This group evidently spent all their money on the P.A. system and didn't have anything left for clothes. I tried hard to think of them as ambassadors for Christ and not merely strange-looking creeps. While the crowd cheered, I tried to bury the thought that representatives of the kingdom of God should at least try for neatness. The cheers turned to pandemonium as they picked up their guitars and started to "rock."

Now I'm a bit hard of hearing, in the habit of making all the old deaf jokes like being deaf in one ear and can't hear out of the other, etc. But now I found myself searching my pockets for something to plug my ears. Little children actually ran screaming from the auditorium holding their ears. The "guitar city" on stage was in full amplified sound and the audience added yells and screams of approval. But I was in a state of shock.

Jesus built His church upon a rock, but I knew it wasn't **this** rock. How could such wildly emotional mayhem possibly achieve the church goal of reaching souls in need of salvation? That had to be just an excuse for this demented entertainment; surely they would not even try to turn it into an evangelistic meeting? I was wrong!

At the end of this ear-bursting concert, the pastor (?) of the sponsoring church got up on the stage and said, "Well, now that you all have heard the gospel, who wants to accept Jesus Christ as their personal Saviour?"

Gospel? What Gospel? I couldn't believe it. I went from shock into catalepsy.

The phony invitational system went into full gear. Selected members of the church started their walk toward the stage to encourage newcomers to make "their decision" for Christ while we all sang "Just As I Am." Many made their "decision" that night.

The next day these brand-new converts came into our store to buy bumper stickers, plastic fish signs, and decals for their car windows. Their interest was not in God, holiness, or the Scriptures, but in "signs" and "trinkets." I began to see how the buying statistics were piling up.

Since we did not wish to sponsor any more "concerts," the "minister of evangelism" decided that he should not support our store any more, so he encouraged others to do the same. Another breach showed in the wall.

I'm glad my wife is not the kind to say "I told you so," although it is amazing how much one can say through speaking Italian eyes.

CHAPTER 11

Play It Again, Sam

I must be a slow learner, or a pushover for a pretty girl, because when Marylou asked me to help her promote **her** concert (she plays the piano and sings), I agreed. Again, all we had to do was put up posters in the windows and pass out free tickets to her debut. My wife rolled her Italian eyes and said, "Here we go again," but I assured her this would not be another fiasco. (After all, what could one girl and one piano do?)

We did our part — up went the posters and we encouraged all our customers to attend. We both knew ol' Marylou. Even though she attended "that" church, she was friendly and sweet and we felt reasonably safe sponsoring her.

The big evening arrived, and the auditorium was filled again (with our help). This time even my wife was there.

I should have known we had come to disasterville when I saw all those electronic trees growing on the stage again. There was a microphone by the piano for Marylou to sing into, and one for the piano. That much I understood. But what were those **two** mikes doing in the set of drums? Was the drummer making a debut also? And the other mikes?

The concert — I should say battle — began. Each guitar tried to play louder than the other. Marylou screamed into the mike to be heard above the rest, and she pounded the piano as loud as she could, but she was no match for the drummer; he was loudest of all. We sat embarrassed; we had invited people to **this.**

But worse was still to come. They introduced a guest musician, a friend from Las Vegas. This was shortly after the murder of John Lennon, and the Las Vegas Christian (?) turned the concert into a memorial for John Lennon of the Beatles. This was the "Lemmon" who had boasted that the Beatles were more popular than Jesus, who had promoted among the youth of our country — drugs, acid rock, protest, and porno music. We were getting "Lemmon" music with "Christian" lyrics; can oil and water mix?

But we still had not run the gamut of the absurd. Into the spotlight walked the pastor (?) of the "Jesus" concert to dedicate the last number to John Lennon — "wherever you are." (Comment withheld.)

When I came to, the seat beside me was empty. My wife had already gone. I looked for a convenience bag under my seat, and finding none, left as quickly as I could. Outside, I took a few deep breaths. After all, I still had to face those loud-speaking Italian eyes.

CHAPTER 12

The Pied-Piper-Pastor

Our store was situated at one end of a little shopping center, which among other advantages, gave us an unlimited private parking area. When a local pastor asked to use our facilities for a central gathering point for his youth group, we were eager to serve.

On the appointed Saturday morning, 60 to 70 young adults gathered in our store. Our cash drawer was delighted; they bought things like 10¢ stickers, 59¢ lapel pins, 98¢ bumper stickers, and some inexpensive $1.98 jewelry. I was pleased to observe their enthusiams, but cringed when they opened their mouths. "Oh, Nancy, look at this little picture of Jesus. Isn't He a cutie?" Or, "Mary, come here. Look at all these crosses! I think I'll come back and get that

one if Bob asks me to the homecoming dance." Another said, "I think I'll buy some of these Christian comics for our house, so my Mom will believe I stopped smoking pot." "Say, mister, you got somethin' that'll make my aunt into a Christian?"

Soon the pastor came in with his youth leaders and gathered the crowd outside into a neat formation. Huge banners were unrolled and placards were distributed. They bowed their heads and prayed in the open parking area. The scene was touching, but I just couldn't put 2 and 2 together. Curiosity got the best of me, and I asked the pastor, "Excuse me, may I ask what you are going to do this morning?"

He replied, "Certainly, praise God, we are going to march all the way into town and then we are going to march all through the downtown area . . . Praise God, we're going to march for Jesus! We're gonna convert our town to Jesus. We're gonna save those pagans by showing them God's love! Isn't that great? Praise, God!" He was babbling. "Here, let me show you." He turned to the group and said, "OK, kids, one practice yell to clear our throats."

"Gimme a J" . . . "J!" . . . "Gimme an E" . . . "E!" . . . "Gimme an S" . . . "S!" . . . "Gimme a U" . . . "U!" . . . "Gimme an S" . . . "S!"

"What does that spell?"

"Jesus! Jesus! J-E-S-U-S, Jesus! Rah! Rah! Rah!"

"OK, kids, let's go! Remember, we're marchin' for Jesus this morning."

With a big "Yea-a-a-a" they went marching off, banners and placards waving. "Gimme a J" . . . "J!"

From the back of the store I heard my wife. "Gimme an A . . . gimme an S . . . a P, an I, an R, an I, an N. What does that spell? ASPIRIN! Quickly!"

She's just not with this modern generation.

CHAPTER 13

Angels Galore

I was intentionally ignoring the notices in our junk mail announcing a new "angel" book. It was advertised as a "must" for all Christian bookstores. But even the brief description of the story turned me off. We had enough "weirdos" sitting on our shelves already, and I was definitely not going to stock this one. Who could possibly want to read it?

When a few orders for the book started coming in, I was not impressed. "A fluke," I assumed. When customers began showing disappointment and irritation because we did not have this book on the shelf, I re-evaluated our position. But this time nearly everybody was talking about angels. Some claimed they knew someone who had just seen some angels and even talked with them. When a pastor came in and ordered a whole case of this book to pass out to his congregation, it finally got my attention. I never sold a case of a title like this before. "I must be missing something," I thought. So I ordered some books for stock, with an extra copy for myself.

So I read it. It made me sick. I thought publishers checked out a story with the Scriptures before they published a "Christian" testimony, but I was wrong! As a novel it would have been bad, but as nonfiction claiming to be the honest-to-God truth, it was a hoax and in bad taste.

The story was about a pastor who was literally visited by two angels, Gabriel and Chironi (probably Moroni's brother angel; Moroni having given Joseph Smith, the Mormon "Golden plates" that countermanded the traditional Word of God). After several angel-homosapien chit-chats, these angels took the pastor on a space flight to the throne room to visit with God Almighty Himself. After talking over old times, the Eternal Creator wrote on a piece of paper some "new revelation," but unfortunately the holy paper turned to ashes when the pastor returned to earth. (Later, even the ashes mysteriously evaporated). That's what happened, honest t' God.

Well, you know me by now. I went straight out and took the remaining copies off the book shelves. "I just can't sell this junk," I said. I had this idea that God was holding me responsible for what I sold over the counter, and that He wouldn't want me selling extra-Biblical experiences to naive spiritual babes, enticing them to believe something contrary to the Scriptures. I was already feeling guilty over some questionable and borderline books in our inventory, and I certainly didn't want to be responsible for passing this lu-lu on to anyone.

The public did not share my sentiments. The disease of "Angelitis" had set in and was spreading. When I tried to point out that we no longer carried the book due to its questionable contents, I was accused of "judging," a new sort of Christian escapism. (Don't the Scriptures tell us to look everything over carefully and reject non-truth?) "No, I'm not judging," I would reply. "I'm not telling you **not** to read the book. If you want it, you can buy it somewhere else, but I simply cannot sell it to you."

We lost many customers over that. We could not be forgiven for our Scriptural convictions. Since the author of the "angel" book was an Assembly of God minister, we were accused of being anti-Assembly. The local Assembly stopped coming in. The scars of their continued unkind remarks toward us we bear to this day.

"Whose idea was it to open this dumb bookstore?" I shouted angrily to my lovely wife.

"Yours, dear," she quietly replied.

"Why do you always listen to me?"

"Because you tell me I have to," she answered softly.

There's just no reasoning with an Italian wife!

CHAPTER 14

Our First — and Last — Christian Booksellers Convention

After twenty-odd years in the furniture and decorating business, I have attended more conventions (called markets in the trade) than I care to remember. To a novice, they are exciting, colorful, fun if noisy, and a chance to see a world prohibited to the eyes of the retail public.

A conducive buying atmosphere is created with gourmet buffets at every corner, supplemented by voluptuous and scantily clad girls passing out freebies, Dixieland bands playing up and down the hallways, clowns, barkers and booze. In every space, from the size of a large room to the size of a large store, you will meet owners, sales-managers, and presidents, plus their local "reps" of the finest lines of home furnishings available in our great nation. Everywhere in this merchandiser's Disneyland are elegant sets of furniture: French Provincial, 18th Century English, Early American, gorgeous upholstery, delicate imported decorator pieces, plush carpets . . . the list is endless.

For the serious, professional buyer, it is tedious and exhausting. He is here, not to admire, but to buy what will sell, to make deals, compare prices and delivery dates, to wrest from this wonderland a good living for himself and his store. At the end of a market day it seems you've walked a hundred miles and spent a million dollars. Many do.

That world was behind me, and I was looking forward to our first CBA (Christian Booksellers Association) convention with anticipation. We had never attended one of these conventions . . . but it would be a gathering of the saints, a convention of those who thought and wrote about God and His Word . . . it would be a chance to participate in a business devoted to promoting the Holy Kingdom of God among His children. I was so eager I could hardly wait for the commuter flight to touch down in Los Angeles.

Alas for my hopes and aspirations. When we arrived, I found it no different than the San Francisco furniture mart during Market Week! Banners, streamers, balloons, blinking signs decorated the center. It was "Temple Time" minus the pigeons. It appeared that all the money-changers from the whole country had come here this day to peddle the Word of God. The atmosphere and the vocabulary were identical to my other past experiences: "Fast mover . . . double your money . . . sells easy . . . quick turnover

. . . now **this** one sells!" **"This** one for your impulse buyer; he won't be able to resist it . . . how many would you like?" The only difference was the product itself.

The expression "Christmas is getting too commercial" is almost like standing on holy ground in comparison to walking through the convention floor.

Displayed from gaily decorated circus booths were things like door mats with the name Jesus to wipe your feet on, Jesus mud-flaps for fenders to collect road dirt, and Christian T-shirts that resembled those one would buy at carnivals and fairs. Books authored by spiritual super-stars were stacked in impressive displays all relating some sort of "Jesus" experience. A little puppy ran by wearing a doggie coat with "Jesus loves me."

"I can't believe this," I said to myself as I tried to listen politely to each factory "rep" that spoke to us. "What are we doing here?" I asked myself. My wife rolled her Italian eyes toward the streamer covered ceiling; she was wondering the same thing.

When you hesitated after a sales presentation with a "Well, I don't know . . . " you heard, "Listen, I'll tell you what. Suppose we give you delayed billing? You won't even get a bill from us for 90 days, then you'll have 30 days after that to pay up. How does that sound? How about a dozen cases? How can you resist a deal like that?" But, since you are being pressured and embarrassed, you say something stupid like, "It's not the money . . . " Ah, the expression changes. "It isn't? Great! Then you can take advantage of our generous prepayment plan. You prepay the invoice and get an additional 10% discount. And since this is a convention special, you get an extra 5% off the top plus our usual 2% 10 net 30. So when you add up all discounts, think what a mark-up you'll have! Think of the money you'll be making in your ministry!" My ministry? I'm feeling rather lost.

Before my wits were collected, a voice at my elbow nearly bowled me over with its vibrant enthusiasm. "Well, hi there, brother! Praise God. Say, I'm sorry I missed you last time I was in your town, praise God, but I had an appointment up north at Brother Bob's Bible Bookstore . . . he had quite an order for me, praise God. Now Brother Bob really buys **big** and moves a lot of merchandise for us, praise God . . . how have you been doing? What was the name of your store again? Oh yes, of course, how could I forget . . . such an unusual name, praise God,; thank you, Jesus and how's your wife, Mary? It's not Mary? Of course, how could I make such a silly mistake as that? Very lovely lady, yes, yes very lovely, praise God. Say, if you have a moment I'd like to show you our new line . . . convention special prices that even **I** can't believe myself . . . take a look at this cute button. Watch how the eyes of Jesus move when you turn and look what it says, 'Jesus has His eyes on you?' Isn't that a great witness? Praise God, everyone will know you're a Christian if you wear a button like this."

I could have told him I had terminal cancer, that I had just buried my wife, and my kids were in jail, but that would not have stopped his sales pitch, praise God and thank you, Jesus. GOODBYE!

That was our first — and last — "selling of Jesus" convention.

CHAPTER 15

Jeu Sells

Mickey Mouse is growing old, Snoopy is slowly losing his touch, E.T. has finally made his phone call and has gone home. Cabbage Patch dolls were harvested too fast to last. But Jeu continues to sell. In fact, JEU is a multi-billion dollar industry, expanding into places where angels (and sober Christians) fear to tread.

With a humble beginning, JEU first entered the plastic and novelty world. In this spiritual five-and-dime store you can buy such items as "holy" combs, nail files or clippers, key chains, balloons, whistles, balls, crickets, pocket knives, hair brushes, plastic cups, sewing kits, and numerous other things (mostly imports from Red China). Somewhere on each item is stamped "Jesus" to make it Christian.

If you fancy spiritual games, there are frisbees, paddle-balls, yo-yos, spin tops, tic-tac-toe boards, puzzles, and so forth. These also are stamped "Jesus" to set them apart from mere worldly yo-yos and frisbees.

In the sanctified stationery department there are "holy" pencils, pens, rulers, letter openers, crayons, book marks, tablets, calendars, greeting and post cards, seals, stickers, badges, ribbons, gift wrap, memo pads, address books, erasers . . . all with "Smile, Jesus loves you" printed on them; thus does an ordinary pencil sharpener become a "Christian" pencil sharpener.

In "Martha's" kitchen department, there are "believer" coffee mugs, tea sets, dishes, coasters, mats, clocks, napkin holders, hot pads, recipe files, trivets, magnets, towels and dish cloths, with the name "Jesus" silk-screened, embroidered, printed or stamped on somewhere to make them suitable for the true Christian home.

For the Christian baby, there are silver spoons (imported from Hong Kong), figurines, toys, lamps, music boxes, stuffed animals, all marked "I'm a Jesus kid."

For the scriptural automobile, there are window decals, Christian mud flaps, dashboard saints, Jesus floor mats, heavenly rear window screens, and Bible bumper stickers that encourage other motorists to "Keep on truckin' with Jesus."

Of course, there is also the Christian clothing department, where overpriced "holy" T-shirts, belts, wallets, purses, ties, sweaters, sport or dress shirts, hats and even **shoe laces** are all embroidered with "Jesus." There is even a jogging outfit so you can jog for "Big J." What a witness!

We all know man cannot live by bread alone, so we combine bread with the Word and it not only sells better, but perhaps even sustains our human system better. In the snack department we have "Christian" instead of Chinese fortune-cookies, Christian-scout cookies, Christian tea bags, Scripture candies and suckers, all sweetly marked, "Jesus loves you."

Added to the usual pictures, mottos, statues and figurines for the home, we now have "Christian" door mats where we can wipe our feet on Jesus before entering the house. We even have "Christian" wallpaper to make our rooms more spiritual. (Guaranteed to drive your neighbors up the wall).

Then the music department, always a financial fortress of solid gains for the stockholders, has been upgraded and expanded. You can now select your favorite Jesus-rock-records from the top 10 or top 40, the list selected by the spiritually deaf.

There's also your favorite aerobic exercise record or cassette for keeping in shape for Jesus. One voice tells you to skip, jump, twist and bend, while a church choir sings "Holy, holy, holy" in the background. You can now hear the Lord's Prayer in a Congo Jungle beat — quite an experience!

Proving Himself a sure seller in every department year after year, JEU has entered big business . . . really BIG. Today you can even buy a JEU franchise! (Yes, they are available, just like McDonald's or Kentucky Fried Chicken), and set up a religious JEU Love Shop in a busy shopping center mall and get in on the big JEU business boom. Money-changers have never had it so good.

Of course, there are still a few wet blankets around (like myself) who feel we owe Sodom and Gomorrah an apology. (Their chief sin, by the way, was not their sexual sin but their greed.)

CHAPTER 16

Who Comes In and What Do They Buy?

Surveys indicate that not more than 10% of active church members ever enter a Christian bookstore. Since many of the people who do come into the store do not buy **books,** one has to wonder what quality of membership we have in the visible church today.

Giving our attention to the active 10% who at least come into the store, what do they buy? I like to think of a Bible Bookstore as an extension of the local church, supplying "meaty" Sunday School literature, supplementing Biblical Sunday sermons with time-tested orthodox reading material, helping the Christian community to "study to show itself approved." But actual sales figures show the following scale of popularity among items offered in the store.

Topping the list are cards and small gifts, mostly cheap jewelry. Next comes what is called "Jesus junk" items like trinkets, bumper-stickers, decals, and toys and plastic prizes for Sunday School. Next comes the latest craze book on "666," giving the month and day of Jesus' return, or the latest out-of-the-body experience testimonials, and a number of "end-time" (mis) interpretations. Next to these are records and cassettes, skimmed-milk devotionals, and low-fat study guides. At the end comes Bibles, reference books, Church History and other serious works. When I opened the store, I actually thought the sequence would be the other way around!

Of the 10% of church members who go to Bible bookstores, only 1% (of the 10%) ever purchase serious books. That means 99% (of the 10%) are satisfied with trinkets or shallow or erroneous writings. I am also told that of the Christian reading public, 85% are women. That boggles my mind and confuses my arithmetic. (I have nothing against women; I just wish the men would read too.)

At first, wanting to think the best, I supposed that perhaps the 90% of the church members, the ones we never see, already own a good library. Maybe they inherited these volumes from some departed saint; maybe they belong to a good Christian book club or send by mail for their reading. Maybe they bought books years ago and now stay home to read their treasures. But alas, I fear that I supposed too much.

After numerous incidents I was forced to conclude that reading good time-tested literature has fallen out of style. In addition to the self-revealing remarks made in the store, I well remember an incident when I was invited to dinner at the home of the head elder in one of the local churches. He was also a successful and prominent businessman, and his lovely home reflected his financial position. He showed me through his home, and all the way I was eagerly looking for his library so I could look over his collection. Bookaholics like myself get our jollies this way! But there did not appear to be one. In fact, I did not even see a book-shelf of any kind. I blurted out:

"Where is your book collection?"

"What book collection?" He sounded a bit surprised.

"I'm sorry, I was just curious to see what you've been reading."

"I don't read. Don't have the time. I'm too busy," he confessed.

"But I thought you were an elder and an adult Sunday School teacher?"

"I am and I do," he stated.

"Then when and how do you prepare for your class?" I asked.

"Oh, I just skim over the notes for the lesson from the teacher's guide right before class."

"I see," I said sadly. What else could I say?

Of course, I didn't really "see." I thought he was a poor excuse for a church leader. Now, if his case was an exception to the norm, I would be horrified. But since I know that he **is** the norm, I am not only horrified, but filled with righteous indignation.

No wonder Christian church members remain in a state of ignorance and are held captive to erroneous teachings. The visible church is void of teachers of the Scriptures. Even if this particular "teaching elder" had studied his leader's guide all week, it is written at a no-fat-milk level. What could he offer to a starved soul? The blind leading the blind is, I am afraid, the in-dictment of today's church.

CHAPTER 17

The Attack of the Bird People

When you are in the people business, you can't help placing certain ones into categories. We did not intend any disrespect nor making fun of people, but our days brought their share of stress and tension, and we needed an "in-house" laugh from time to time to keep us in perspective. One of these in-house jokes was my answer to my wife's question, "How are we doing this morning?" I would answer, "One St. James, two late-greats, and some bird people." Decoded, this means a first time customer who asked for a "St. James Bible," two customers who wanted the "Late Great Planet Earth," and the others thought they were looking at Jonathan Livingston Seagull on a gold pendant.

It never ceased to amaze me that people who claimed to be long-time Christians, who claimed active church membership, who even claimed to be Bible-study teachers, could look down into our jewelry case and ask, "What's that six-pointed star stand for?" or "What do those flames mean? . . . What does the lamb represent?" and even, "What's that bird?"

Not knowing Christian symbols is certainly no crime, but some of the questions were ludicrous. For example, it is quite normal for a young child to ask, "Where do babies come from?" But if a young, married adult asked the same question, there would be eyebrows raised. A babe in Christ would not be expected to know the significance of the lamb symbol, or the meaning of the flame that appeared above the heads of those in the upper room at Pentecost. They might not even know the symbol of the Holy Spirit as a dove. But after a few years down the road, one might question what's going on when those things are unrecognized by a middle-aged Christian, especially after he has just informed you of his Church activities and "spiritual" achievements.

It was common for people to come into the store and want to "share"—which usually meant bragging about their religious achievements. It seems they had done "it" better, longer, and in higher quality than us "regular" Christians. But then they would ask "the question:" "By the way, what's that bird stand for?"

Some spoke only by chapter and verse. They didn't repeat the verse, but they quoted the chapter and verse reference as if we had all memorized the same scriptures as themselves. "I was praying in the Spirit this morning, and the Lord impressed me with Isaiah 59:19, Mark 13:11, and Jude 19 and 20. What do you think of those verses?" Oh, dear. They were disappointed, dismayed, even shocked when I admitted that I was not familiar with the particular passage.

"That's too bad. Well, maybe someday the Lord will give you the spiritual insight that He has given me. Praise God! You're not baptized in the Holy Ghost, are you? I can tell. Oh, it's such a wonderful experience. It's deep. I mean d-e-e-p. Oh, by the way, how much is that cute bird on the gold plate? And what does it mean?"

CHAPTER 18

Conversations Over the Counter

Before I got into the Bible Bookstore business, I somehow assumed that all people had the same respect and awe that I had been brought up to have for the book of all books, the Bible. I also thought that all people had some idea of what this Book was supposed to be . . . but I assumed too much. The following are some actual conversations that took place over my Bible counter. The people must have had some kind of God-consciousness, or they would not have been in the store. But I can't help wondering . . . what is happening in the minds of people today?

"You look upset. How can I help you?"

"I'm sorry. I've just come from the hospital, where I learned that my mother has cancer and she doesn't have long to live. I'd like to buy her a Bible."

"Do you know what kind your mother would like?"

"Yes. Something that isn't too religious."

"Good morning. May I be of help?"

"Yes, I'd like to buy a Bible."

"Did you have a particular one in mind?"

"Yes. I want the same one Jesus used. I don't want any of those new translations."

"Good morning ....."

"Yes, I bought this Bible here, and I'd like to return it and get my money back."

"Is something wrong?"

"Yes, it didn't work."

"It didn't work?"

"Yes, I gave it to my mother because she was very sick, but she died anyhow."

"I'm sorry ... "

Presumably, people who read the Bible must also go to church. But if that is the case, then what is happening in the churches of today?

"Good afternoon, madam. May I help you?"

"I'd like to replace my old Bible. I haven't had it too long, but it's just falling apart. I guess I just used it too much. Anyhow, I'd like to get one just like it."

"Yes, ma'am. What kind was it?"

"What kind?"

"I meant to say, is it a King James Version, New American Standard, Revised ... "

"I don't know what you mean. It's just a Bible . . . a Bible."

"I'm sorry, I should have asked you which translation it was."

"Translation? Well, in English of course. Land sakes, I got enough problems readin' English without bothering with them foreign languages. There it is! The one right over there. Mine has a black cover just like that, 'cept mine is all wore out."

"I'm glad we had what you wanted, ma'am."

"I'd like to buy a Bible."

"Certainly. What kind would you like?"

"A Saint James edition please."

"Could you be meaning the King James version?"

"No, I want a **Saint** James version. You know, the one with all those thees and thous, the one that has John 3:16 in it."

"Yes, ma'am, I know exactly which one you are referring to. Let's see John 1,2,3, . . . there it is. Is this the one you want?"

"Let's see, 14,15,16 . . . 'For God so loved the world . . .' Yep. That's the one. I just knew you would have a copy."

"Thank you. I'm glad we did."

"Yes, ma'am. May I help you?"

"Yes, I'd like to buy a **holy** Bible."

"Yes, ma'am, we don't carry any other kind."

"I think you are mistaken. This one is just a regular Bible and I want to buy a **holy** Bible."

"A regular Bible?"

"Yes, it does not say 'Holy' on the cover. I insist on buying only a **Holy** Bible. I'm very religious, you know."

"Yes ma'am. I recognized that right away."

"Hello, there. How are you?"

"Just fine, thank you. But I'd like to return this Bible."

"Oh. What seems to be the problem?"

"I precisely asked you for a red-letter edition and you went and sold me a black-letter edition."

"I did? I'm sorry. May I please see the Bible?"

"Certainly. See. Page after page after page, and no red letters!"

"Yes, ma'am. You're in the Old Testament portion. A red-letter edition indicates all the words that Christ spoke, and they're in the New Testament only."

"Well, didn't He talk in the Old Testament?"

"Yes, ma'am. The whole Bible is the Word of God. A red-letter Bible, that is, the New Testament portion, merely indicates the words that Jesus spoke while He was on earth."

"What difference does that make, if He's here on earth or up in heaven? I just want to read the words of God."

"You've got it in your hands now, ma'am. Just start reading. You can't go wrong."

One discontented customer had my full sympathy.

"I'd like to return this Bible. It's defective."

"Defective. I'm sorry. Where?"

"The concordance in the back must be half missing."

"Hmmm. It seems all right. All the pages are there."

"Well, something must be wrong, because the word I'd be looking for is never there."

Another had a very common problem:

"Yes, sir, may I help you?"

"Yes, I'd like a pocket Bible to fit in my shirt pocket here."

"Do you want the complete Bible or just a New Testament?"

"Oh, I want the whole Bible, from Genesis to Revelation."

"The smallest one we have is this one; it will fit in

your shirt pocket and it's in very durable leather."

"Great! That is just the right size. Wait a minute! I can't read this! The print is too small! Don't you have one with larger print?"

"No, sir. A Bible that size will always come in that tiny print."

"Well, I certainly don't have any trouble reading the Bible I got now."

"What's wrong with the one you have?"

"It won't fit in my shirt pocket."

"Oh."

"Yes, ma'am, may I show you any particular Bible?"

"I'd like to see a copy of the New International American Revised Version please."

"Which one was that again, ma'am?"

"You know, the easy-to-read version. I've tried all the others and I just can't understand a single word."

"I'd be surprised if you did, ma'am."

Not all the conversations were like these. Many were meaningful and spiritually uplifting. One person asked me if I would "bless" his Bible, and I told him they were already blessed by the Master. There were many opportunities to share, to teach, to help and to be helped, to pray, to love, to be enriched. Some of the conversations make me feel good even to this day. We paid a tremendous price for what we thought of as our ministry, but it was worthwhile. If we still chuckle over some of the conversations, it is only to ease the heartache over the great needs, and the pride and prejudice of the visible church in our small town that finally intentionally annihilated our ministry.

On a slow day, with the rent due, what is one to do except see the humor in conversations like this one:

"Yes, ma'am, how may I help you this morning?"

"I'd like to have a hundred Bibles so I may pass them out."

"A hundred! In that case, to keep the cost down, may I recommend this paperback edition . . . "

"Sir, I do not want to pass out cheap copies. I'd like something nice."

"Well, then, may I suggest this sturdy cloth edition . . ."

"No, no, no! I said something 'nice' and I want something nice like that pretty one over there."

"You have excellent taste, madam. Yes, this is a beautiful edition. But this is deluxe top-grain cowhide and sells for $69.95. Do you realize how much one hundred of these will cost you?"

"Cost me? You mean I have to pay you for them even though I'm going to be giving them away?"

"I'm afraid so, ma'am."

"I thought God's Word is supposed to be free."

"It is, ma'am. You are only paying for the ink, the paper, the leather, the man who prints and the man who brings it to our door. Have you tried contacting one of the Bible societies?"

"Yes, I have, but they won't ship me what I want until I send them a check."

"What is this world coming to!"

CHAPTER 19

This Is God Speaking

In our town, we saw many customers frequently (at least until we were boycotted), and it became natural to have conversations and even prayers together. Many customers came to buy books that had been recommended by a friend, and they asked our opinion of the book. They also told us things their pastor had said to them and again asked our opinion. We were continually shocked at how often the preferred book or the pastor's statements were unbiblical.

My standard reply was, "I don't think you really want my opinion, because that is all it would be — my opinion. But I would be happy to share with you what the Bible states on the subject." I was surprised to learn that most people did not want to hear what the

Great Text said: they were just curious to know what I thought of certain matters. No matter how carefully I emphasized that I was quoting the Bible, they repeated it to each other as "he said." Then other people would take me to task for contradicting their pastor. I was considered a dissension maker and "anti" toward the denomination the pastor represented.

At this time there was great excitement at one church. The pastor was receiving "new revelations" from God. There are, of course, many denominations today that believe in such new words from the Lord. I have no real quarrel with this belief, but I personally would like to compare the new word with the old Word to see if they agree. In most of these messages it is interesting to note that God is still speaking Elizabethan English.

The current wave of prophetic messages from God was unique. The message was not the usual speaking in tongues, or a simple verbal prophetic word; it wasn't even in archaic English. The message came via the pastor's typewriter and was mimeographed for the congregation.

This is God the Father speaking, and I quote:

"I like you. I like your style, although it is a bit sloppy . . . Why don't some of you learn to sing parts? I like four-part harmony . . . What I don't like is your complaining about the church and its leaders. If you don't like the worship or the parking . . . stop griping. You are out of line . . . give Me 300 committed ministers and I will perform miracles that will cause the name of Jesus and also_____(name withheld) Community Church to be famous . . . We will have to do this again sometime . . . Please talk about what I said . . . I want to know if you intend to do anything which I have suggested. (Signed) Your Loving Father." (There was a lot more in similar vein.)

Several copies of this "message from God" showed up on my counter, put there by excited church members who either wanted my approval or just to share their current ecstasy. God was speaking to them, God was going to make Jesus and them famous, and they were asking me, "Isn't that exciting news?" I admitted it was a pretty hard act to follow, but requested time to look over the "message" before I replied.

So many copies of this strange message had been put on my counter that I thought I should mimeograph my own reply. I put down some Scriptures, and, yes, I even threw in my own "opinion." I couldn't help questioning the stability of a minister who would claim from the pulpit that he got such a message from God — "Stop griping! I'm gonna make Jesus and you famous! . . . Your singing is sloppy . . . "

It might as well have been headlines in the newspaper: "Bookstore owner calls pastor quack." I really didn't say that. On second thought, maybe I did think he was a quack, and my feelings came through in my words. Anyway, another segment of the community was alienated.

My beautiful wife was walking around the store with her feather duster, dusting the books that had already been dusted so often — Bunyan, Luther, Edwards, Spurgeon, Schaeffer, Murray, Ryle, Packer, and so on. All the greats, the vitals, the traditional and accepted authors sat on the shelves untouched, collecting dust. Even when I explained to people what these time-tested books were, they rejected them in favor of some current "off-the-wall" testimony.

I called out to my wife, "Why did we buy all these books?"

She waved her feather scepter and answered, "Because you like to see me dust?"

CHAPTER 20

Openers and Mind Blowers

One never knew, when we arrived at the store in the morning, what the day would bring; but funny or sad, it always brought something unexpected.

One morning just before opening time I was vacuuming the carpet when a car pulled into our lot and a distressed looking woman got out and rushed up to the front door. She stopped to read our sign on the door giving our hours, checked with her watch, looked glum and started back to her car. I was concerned about her tormented condition, so I dropped the vacuum and rushed out the door.

"Hello! I'm here. Can I help you?"

"Oh, thank God, you're open," she cried, rushing back.

I got behind the counter and beamed at her. It always makes you feel good to be helpful first thing in the morning.

"Yes. Now what can I do for you?"

"Oh, God. Just tell me where you keep your aspirin."

"Aspirin? I'm sorry, I don't have any aspirin."

"You don't carry aspirin! What kind of a grocery store is this?"

"Grocery store? This isn't a grocery store. It's a Christian bookstore."

"It's a wha . . . Oh, God! I'm worse off than I thought."

She ran out the door, holding her head, jumped into her car and drove off.

If some of our more inventive religious entrepreneurs had only thought to make a Gospel aspirin with "JESUS LOVES YOU" stamped on it, perhaps I could have ministered to that poor woman!

Our most unforgettable customers drove up at closing time one day. The story is so bizarre that I would not dare tell it except that it has to be true because no one could have ever imagined anything so strange.

I was just locking up when a souped-up jeep pulled up right behind me. This jeep was "loaded," with a giant antenna waving in the air, all kinds of spotlights mounted on top, a P.A. speaker and complete stereo system, plus anything else one would need for an extended safari expedition. Two men sat inside.

"Hey, brother," one called, "Can ya' com'ere a minute?"

"Certainly," I replied, "How can I help you?"

"It's kinda hard for us to get around," he said, "do ya' mind given' us curb service?"

I noticed two sets of crutches lying on the floor, and both men appeared to be amputees.

"We need a half-dozen Gospel 8-track tapes," one said.

"Any particular ones?" I inquired. "Do you have any favorites?"

"Naw, just some ol' fashioned Gospel hymns. Give us six good ones. Here's the money; keep the change."

That sort of thing didn't happen often! I brought out six tapes which I considered to be the best of what I had in stock and handed them to the men. I happened to look down and noticed that between the front seats, along with the crutches, lay several high-powered rifles. My curiosity got the best of me. Hunters on crutches?

"Excuse me, gentlemen, may I ask you . . . ?"

The driver could see how puzzled I looked and interrupted with an answer. "Oh, we're just missionaries on our way to Mexico."

"Missionaries? Then why the rifles?"

"Well you see, we have a very unusual sort of ministry. What we do is drive to some remote village and turn on the P.A. system full-blast with some good ol' Gospel music. When the dumb spiks come out of their huts to see what the noise is all about, we preach 'em the Gospel. If they reject our message, we ventilate their Mexican hides with these babies," and he patted the rifles with his hand. "You see, we get 'em in the kingdom one way or t'other."

"Isn't murder against God's law?" I asked.

"Naw. We see it as mercy killin'. We just nudge 'em into the kingdom just a bit sooner than they expected to go, that's all." With a roar of a powerful engine, their oversized tires spun on the asphalt and they drove off.

My "Vayan con Dios" was spoken to empty air. Their money was burning my conscience, but I had been too dumbfounded to do or say anything to them.

My wife simply wasn't going to believe this one.

CHAPTER 21

Is This For Real?

There is no way for me to know the original intents of the founders of today's Christian publishing houses. I suspect that many of them truly intended to honor the Lord. But all I know for sure is what is happening today under the banner of Christianity.

Too many Christian publishers have long ago been bought out by large, secular corporations. JEU means money, and the smart boys know it. It is common knowledge, for example, that one of the biggest Christian publishers has been bought out and is owned by ABC (American Broadcasting Company). The responsibility of ABC or any corporation is to show a profit to its stockholders. People invest money to make money, not to support a cause. The officers of the company are there to insure that the investors make money. They are interested only in "winners" that move fast and in large numbers. A "loser" is a slow mover and is scrapped instantly. The question is not, "Is it Christian?" or "Will it help Christians?" but "Will it sell?" The results of this commercial approach to Christian publishing is sometimes funny, but more often sad.

A lady came into the store, explained that her nerves were shot, and she wanted some soft and soothing Christian music. Without hesitation I suggested a "Praise" cassette, the latest in a series of Praise albums with which I was familiar. I had found them to be fine music and just what I thought she was asking for. I placed a factory-sealed tape in her shaking hands and she left.

In a short while she returned, furious. She had trusted me; why had I sold her such an awful tape? "Do you make a practice of playing cruel jokes on defenseless people?" she asked. I let her express herself without interruption; it seemed best in her state to let her ventilate all her disappointment. I made my sincerest and deepest apologies, assuring her that I was equally confused in her disappointment. I confessed that I had not personally listened to this particular tape, as it had just come in this morning, but as it was the latest in a series of Praise albums with which I was familiar, I had assumed it was the same. I gave her some older tapes that I **knew** were safe choices and took back the one she returned.

The cover on the tape showed a beautiful mountain and seemed typical of the series. It was clearly marked "Praise." Perhaps the lady was too particular?

At home that evening I gave the tape to my teenaged son to see what he thought of it. "Aw, Dad, not

'Praise,'" he objected.

But I insisted, so he took it upstairs to check it out. After a while he came back and exclaimed, "Hey, Dad, I didn't know Christians went in for acid-rock."

I exclaimed, "What are you talking about?"

He answered, "This is A/C-D/C. Are you sure you should be selling this stuff in your store?"

Sure enough, it was A/C-D/C, a popular acid rock group — which I feel is demonic — on a tape clearly labeled "Praise." It was manufactured by a Christian publisher. How did it get there? Was it a mistake at the production plant? Or was it another case of a Christian company selling out to "what will sell," instead of what is Christian and moral. I had seen so many examples of "Christian" companies leaving Christianity behind in an effort to make a profit for their investors that I was ready to believe anything.

Another lady brought back a Christian devotional book that she had just purchased. Half-way through, it became "Lord of the Flies." The two were bound together under one cover. There was one publisher, but two ideologies. Does it take "Flies," which is against all that Christianity stands for, to make a buck for the investors?

Yet another lady brought a book into the store for me to examine. A clerk from another Christian bookstore highly recommended it to her, but she had her misgivings and wanted my opinion. The publisher was one of the largest in the industry. The "key" to the book was to learn the fact that "you are God." The author claimed that if anyone will accept this "towering truth of universal consciousness," it will be revealed to him that "You are not just part of God; you are altogether God, and God is altogether you." The author proves his theory with quotations from the Upanishads (a Hindu philosophy), from the Vedanta (the worship of the Hindu god Brahma), and also from Jesus (selected texts only). This book came from the printing presses of a "Christian publisher" and sold in "Christian" bookstores. Does Hinduism sell better than Christianity?

Our daughter was expecting her first baby, and my wife selected a book from our shelves on "expecting" and sent it to her. We had not read it — we did not have time to read every book that came in, and we were not expecting, so it was not on our reading list. We just thought it would be an appropriate gift from a Christian bookstore owner to his daughter — until we got the phone call.

"Why did you send me such a terrible book?"

"Terrible! What's wrong with it? We've sold lots of copies and not one has complained, so what's with you?"

"Well, the book claims that God is a 'she.'"

"God is what?"

"Yep. The author says that we are all wrong in assuming God is a 'he.' Since all life is born from woman, therefore God must be a 'she.'"

We were speechless. We really didn't want to believe her, but she mailed the book back to us, and that's exactly what it said. Yet this book was published by one of the more conservative Christian publishers.

We wondered why none of the people who bought the book ever said anything to us. Were they so offended by the book that they never came back? Or . . . did they agree with it?

As I was pondering these questions, the only positive thought that came from my wife was that she was very thankful it was not she who was "expecting."

CHAPTER 22

Sued For a Cool Million

Before I knew what was happening to me, I was in the cardiac intensive care unit. I was in bed and surrounded by people. One injected something into my arm, another taped tubing into my nose and turned on the oxygen valve. One took my blood pressure, another pushed a needle connected to an I.V. bottle into my arm. The doctor listened through his stethoscope, another nurse attached a bunch of wires to my body, connecting me to a green TV screen. I watched a little speck go "bleep, bleep" up and down the monitor.

Never in my life had I been given so much attention; I felt sort of guilty. Why all this commotion and concern over me? They kept on repeating, "Just relax, you're going to be OK, you're going to be OK."

The thought of **not** being OK had not crossed my mind. I didn't even know what I was doing here. I knew I didn't feel good, it was hard to breathe, and I had a pain in my chest, but I had felt worse things before. Why are they saying, "I'm going to be OK?" Does that mean I might **not** be OK?

After another injection, I felt light and airy, and oh, so "relaxed." At first I thought I was going to have one of those "out-of-the-body" experiences. But no, I was just getting "high," and I kept smiling at everyone, even though they continued in a serious manner while moving at precision speed.

I stopped smiling when I recalled the incident that brought me here:

A man came into the store claiming to be a Christian representing a group of Christian investors from the Bay Area and wanted to know my first-hand opinion about a certain local "ministry." Little did I know that he was actually sent in to set me up and that he had a hidden microphone that recorded our whole conversation. Since he claimed concern over a possible loan for a very large sum of money, I answered all of his questions honestly. My comments needed no exaggeration as the "ministry" in question had long condemned itself. The next thing I knew, a process server handed me a million dollar slander law suit! The day after giving my deposition I was rushed to the hospital.

I could not stop my flesh from being angry, resentful, and bitter. How could a so-called "professing" Christian, one who even claims to be a minister, create such a malicious and intentionally fraudulent situation that would put me here? The legal fees of the law suit to defend myself were already beyond my ability to pay, and now the hospital bill! While my flesh cried out for revenge, the Words of God kept repeating in my mind. "All things work together for good. All things work together for good. All things work . . . "

I wondered what "good" could come out of being a victim of entrapment (as the deposition proved), tricked into the hands of an evil man to further his mad obsession for filthy lucre and throwing me into such debt. This man has sued more people, organizations, newspapers and even motion picture studios, than the county clerk cares to count. Has he ripped I Cor. 6:1-8 out of his Bible? How did I ever get involved in this million dollar law suit? Soon the sedation took effect and gladly forgetting everything, I fell asleep.

The next day I had an unusual experience when a friend came to visit me. He was talking and watching the green monitor at the same time (as it is quite fascinating). Suddenly his expression changed from smiles and encouragement to a look of deep concern, if not shock. I turned to see what was causing his terror and the TV screen was no longer rhythmically bleeping. Instead, it was one long straight line of b-e-e-e-p. I could not believe my eyes; I was dead and did not even know it! In fact, I didn't even feel different. I saw the nurses come running from their central control island. They frantically looked, poked, lifted, and discovered the problem: by my moving around in bed I had disconnected myself from the monitor. I wasn't dead after all.

The rest of the day I just watched the monitor, knowing that every "bleep" was a heartbeat. It is a fearful thing to watch, knowing that if that little ball stops bouncing, that's it! I'm dead! New thoughts, yet not really new, crowded my mind. Supposen' I do die, what then? What will it be like? Do I have anything to worry about? Of course not, I told myself. "I am a

Christian." I kept repeating that, but when the flesh is exposed to a crisis, it will always revert back to "self." Our carnal natures will momentarily take the upper hand and convince us that "all is well." My natural mind did the very thing I had promised myself so many times I would never do.

To convince myself that I had no "worries" in entering the next life, I did a foolish thing: I looked to **myself!** "Of course I have no worries," I assured myself. I am an ordained minister. I own a Christian bookstore. I write Gospel tracts. My theology is orthodox-reformed. You can't get closer to the truth than that! I might as well have been reciting Matthew 7:22 to God. "Lord, haven't I done marvelous works in Your Name? Lord, haven't I even cast out demons in Your Name?" I, I, I, . . . I was looking to myself and of all things, I was pleased! Then all of a sudden it happened! The truth replaced my favorable evaluation of my life. My sins rose up against me and damned me. My numberless, countless sins stood before me and condemned me. I could not get rid of them, for I saw that I and my sins were one. I could not separate myself from myself! I could not separate myself from sin. We were one!

I saw that everything in me, from me, was nothing but sin. My very best, my "holiness" was still sin in the eyes of Him who was about to judge me. My whole life, my very breath was sin. Not one good thing dwelt in me, nor could I even do one thing that was not sin in the eyes of the Holy One. I was chained to myself and I fell back in bed in total despair, a damned human.

I realized that before I was even born, I was damned. And, the longer I lived, the more I damned myself. I looked back across the centuries and saw that I was actually damned in Eden. I was condemned with Adam, because I was **in** Adam; there exists a perfect solidarity between Adam and me. I stood with Adam and rebelled against my Creator with him. "We are all doomed," I cried. The whole human race is damned!

The situation seemed hopeless. Scriptures appeared in my mind as if on a computer screen. "**All** had sinned" "**All** come short of the Glory of God." "**No one** is righteous, no not even one." "**No one** seeks after God." "**All** have gone their own way." "Oh, wretched man that I am. Who will deliver me from this body of sin and death? Who will deliver me from myself?" Even though I **knew** the answer, I did not know the answer. I moaned, "Oh Lord, I **do** believe. Help thou my unbelief."

When I stopped looking to myself, peace finally returned to my soul. I was now looking where I should: **outside myself!** I was now looking to Him who I could really depend on: my Substitute! Oh, thanks be to God, I **have** a Substitute! Never had the absolute necessity and the infinite blessing of the Substitute been so perfectly clear.

What joy unspeakable to return to the Apostolic faith of our fathers, even from a moment of doubt or unbelief. That "moment" seemed like eternity. I wonder what real eternity will be like? What terror must strike the souls of those who are never saved when they wake up on the other side engulfed in total darkness and silence, where the only sound they will ever hear is the agonizing scream of their own voice and the gnashing of teeth? Oh, what a terrible thought!

Since that day when I was wheeled into that cardiac intensive care unit, recovery has been slow and medical bills keep mounting. Shortly I will begin a new treatment that is promised to help me regain my physical health, but this will put me even further in debt. My thoughts turn to the cause of my misfortune and again my flesh crawls with anger. How many times have I recited our Pledge of Allegiance that ends with the words: "and justice for all." "This is not justice," I say. "This is mockery of justice." "It is not only illegal, but immoral!" I declare.

Under the advice of his attorney, my accuser withdrew the law suit against me with the condition that I agree not to press charges against him; that I would not sue him for malicious persecution. Compelled by the Words of God — "Vengeance is **Mine,** saith the Lord. I **will** repay," — I signed the agreement.

My wife and our friends kept the store going in my absence. People coming in wanted to know what really happened, as my unfortunate experience was only part of a multi-million dollar law suit involving a newspaper that was running an exposé on this "ministry." By now the story was getting national coverage. My wife and I vowed not to speak to anyone regarding this matter, which included the many visiting reporters who wanted "a story." One trip to the cardiac intensive care unit in a life time is once too many. Who said a bookstore is boring? "Yes, sir, may I help you? You want inside information on what? Never heard of it!"

CHAPTER 23

The Inquisition

Through our display windows, I saw a large, modern car pull into our parking lot and four ladies from St. Michael's* got out. They came inside immediately and began making selections, while the driver remained outside to finish a cigarette. When he came in, I recognized Father Jones* from our local Catholic parish. As the ladies stacked up many books on our sales counter, Father Jones marched up and down the aisles like a man on a mission. He seemed to know what he wanted, but didn't know where it was.

He finally spotted what he was apparently looking for, the book "Roman Catholicism" by Boettner (Presbyterian & Reformed Publisher) and "The Two

*Names have been changed to protect the innocent: us!

Babylons" by Hislop (Loizeaux Publishers). He summoned the ladies and began reading excerpts to them. Then he pointed out other books, all by respected Protestant publishers: "Mystery Babylon" by Woodrow, "So What's the Difference" by Ridenhour (Gospel Light Publishers), "Council of Trent" by Chemnitz (Concordia Publishers), "Secrets of Romanism" by Zaccello (Loizeaux Publishers), "Vatican II" (Eerdmans Publishers), and others, including books by Luther, Calvin, John Owen.

He dismissed the ladies to continue their shopping and turned toward me. "You," he commanded sternly. "Come here."

I smiled and tried a cheerful "Good morning, how can I help you?"

"Get those books off the shelf!" he demanded.

Taken aback, I thought perhaps I misunderstood. "I beg your pardon?" I said.

"You heard me. Get these books off the shelf. Now!"

Trying to keep my composure, I politely tried to explain our store policy, which was that since we could not read every book that came in, we welcomed and appreciated our customers bringing to our attention any book that was unscriptural. If we found this to be true, we removed it at once. But the books he showed me were ones with which I was familiar. In fact, I called them our "meat department," our reference and doctrinal books, commentaries, church histories, etc. These books, I told him, were personally found to be scripturally sound.

He was not mollified. "Look mister, this trash is an embarrassment to our church, and I'm telling you to get these books off the shelf immediately!" He actually poked a finger toward my chest!

This was no longer a customer-salesman conversation. To put it bluntly, I lost my cool. I entirely forgot that the "customer is always right." So I answered, "Look, I'm not one of your parishioners; don't come into my store and lay some power-trip on me. You're not my pope."

He wasn't listening. "I don't think you understand me. If you don't remove these books right now, we will no longer buy from this store."

"That, sir, is your privilege, but those books stay," I answered and walked back to the counter.

He whispered to one of the ladies who was still browsing and had appeared to ignore our confrontation. He then left the store and went out to sit in the car. Time passed and the ladies stacked still more books on the counter. But I had a sinking premonition of what was coming, and it came.

The group finally approached with their last selections, and I asked, "Will this be all for you ladies this morning?"

"Yes . . . but you see, we have a wee bit of a problem. We would like to buy all these books from you today, but Father Jones brought to our attention that you carry some anti-Catholic literature here. Unless you promise not to sell such things any more, not only will we not be able to buy these books today, we won't be able to ever buy here again."

"I'm sorry to hear that, ladies," I replied, "but I wish to point out, if I may, that the reference books you refer to have been here since the day we opened. We've always carried them. But that hasn't hindered our relationship in the past. Haven't I always served you ladies politely and in love? Haven't I spent time with each of you individually, trying to assist you in finding just the 'right' book? Haven't we even prayed together, right here in this store, over some of your personal problems?"

"Oh . . . you, you've always been very nice. But you

see, Father Jones said that unless . . . "

I interrupted, "Ladies, I **am** very sorry, but I can't change history. I cannot change what is true. Nor will I be intimidated or blackmailed! These books must stay on the shelf unless you can prove them to be in error Biblically. No . . . don't bother, I'll return these books to their places. I understand your position. I just hope you understand mine."

So they got into the car with Father Jones and drove away.

A few days later a familiar Lutheran priest came running in the door, "What's going on in here? What are you doing?" he inquired anxiously.

I could not imagine what could have put him into such a state of agitation. "I'm sorry, but I don't know what you're talking about," I said with concern.

"What do you mean, you don't know? I just had a long talk with Father Jones and he informed me that your store is loaded with anti-Catholic literature, and that you are creating a division in our Christian community. You know I'm in charge of the ecumenical movement in this town, and I'm trying to get people to put aside their differences. And here you are, undermining my work. What are you trying to do, ruin everything?"

So I told him exactly what had happened, including the "big ultimatum," and asked if he felt that I should also remove all books on the Reformation. He did not answer. Trying to better illustrate my position, I asked, "How would you personally feel if someone demanded that I remove 'Bondage of the Will' from the shelf?"

"'Bondage of the Will?' What's that?" he asked.

I could not credit my ears. A Lutheran, a priest at that, and he did not know Martin Luther's most famous book! Is this possible? Scarcely knowing whether to treat him as simply ignorant or a religious imposter, I tried to explain myself, and ended by saying that a mixture of truth and error only produces mud.

In a few days, the big parade began. Every day someone would come in with an "Oh, how could you?" remark. "We Catholics are Christian just like you. How could you carry those terrible books . . . and in a **Christian** bookstore?" We kept asking them to show us where these books were in error, but they refused to discuss either history or the Scriptures.

Obviously, some were sincere — that is, sincerely ignorant of the truth. But most said the same thing, almost word for word, like a carefully prepared statement. Some tried to bait us into some incriminating conversation. To avoid repetition of idle talk as a waste of time, I wrote several tracts. In them I gave some historical data and showed the difference between the Roman Catholic religion and the Protestant view of Christianity. This only created a bigger problem. Now, I was accused of actively passing out anti-Catholic hate material. I couldn't win.

St. Michael's put notices in their Sunday bulletins that our store was strictly off limits to all good Catholics. It was suggested to us that we should file a legal restraint of trade suit against them, but I felt this would be wrong. We did not want trouble; all we wanted to do was to bring good literature and truth to the Christian community, regardless of which "box" they fitted into on Sundays. We never pushed what we knew to be truth on anybody, simply made it available for those who wanted it.

On another occasion, a group of young men came into our store and headed straight for our "meat department" where the "anti-Catholic" books were on view. They began making negative comments in voices to be heard throughout the store. They could not have been more obnoxious if they tried. This was not a motorcycle gang, but well-dressed, well-groomed young adults. The gist of their remarks seemed to be "We are Catholics and we hate your guts!" Their "Roman" cheer on the way out, was "Someone ought to throw a bomb in this store!"

Two ladies present in the store shook their heads, smiled at us in pity, and asked, "Do you think they were Catholics?"

As fate would have it, right at this time a major Sacramento newspaper ran a big story on the "Crusaders" series published by Chick Publications. (Sacramento is only twenty miles away from our smaller town.) This created an interest in our revolving rack holding Chick tracts. It used to sit peacefully and quietly in a corner, out of the mainstream but available for those who enjoyed this form of publication. The news that we carried Chick material went around, and soon a new barrage of "Oh, how could you?" accusations were showered upon us.

I got tired of people walking in to ask if we carried "Alberto" because when I said, "Yes, we do," they snarled, "And you call yourself Christian!" walking out in a huff. So I moved the Chick rack right up by the front door so they wouldn't have to ask for "Alberto." There it is! If they didn't like it, they didn't have to come any further. (Many Christian bookstores handle Chick publications in an "under the counter" manner). The paradox was that the majority of people who were creating an issue over Chick comics were strangers to us who had never patronized our store. It appeared they were sent to harass us.

One day a gentleman I had never seen before casually approached me. He was polite and complimentary on the store. After some small talk, he came to the point. He took a Chick Crusader from his pocket and told me his son had bought this from us, and he was extremely upset. He asked me if I agreed with the contents, as he turned page after page which were heavily underlined.

"My goodness," I said, "you have so many places underlined. May I answer them one at a . . . ?"

But his composure was gone. He interrupted me shouting, "Look, I'm a Catholic. Maybe not a good one, but I'm still a Catholic. And I don't like my kid coming home with this kind of trash from this place! Now, do you or do you not agree with the contents of this hate magazine?"

"I'm sorry that you are upset," I answered. "May I try to clear up this matter? Please point to any specific statement in the magazine with which you disagree and I will answer you honestly."

He opened the folded publication and pointed to an underlined statement at random. I read it and said, "Well, sir, I am aware that the Roman Catholic religion openly teaches this, but you see, the Bible very clearly states that . . . "

"Never mind," he interrupted, "I see where you're coming from now, and I'm going to fix you but good."

He spoke his name to me as if I should know it. I didn't. Since I did not know him, he informed me that he was a very influential writer for a Sacramento newspaper and that he had many influential friends. I said I was happy for him.

He answered, "Well, you won't be happy for long, buddy," he exploded. "I'm going to call a special meeting of the ministerial association up here, and we're going to close you down! I'm going to make sure that every church in town boycotts this store!"

"That's a pretty heavy duty threat from a person who claims to be a loving Catholic," I said. I'm afraid I said it with some sarcasm.

"This is no idle threat, buddy! You'll see!" and he stormed out the door.

At this point I could only look upward and say, "Oh, Lord," as if God were hiding behind the florescent fixtures, "are you sure about all this? You must admit, Lord, it's getting kind of hairy down here. In fact, I think it's getting out of hand."

The Scriptures came to me, the **promise** of persecution (II Tim. 3:12) and the **identification** of the persecutors: the visible church (John 16:2-3).

Sure enough, it had been no idle threat. One by one, the local churches withdrew their support without explanation. They traveled over twenty miles to the next nearest Christian bookstore for their needs rather than give us their business.

In sincere sadness and concern, I can only remind those who have openly hurt us and have gone to so much time, trouble and money to silence us, of this passage: "He who saith he is in the light, and hateth his brother, is in darkness even until now . . . he that hateth his brother is in darkness, and walketh in darkness, and knoweth not whither he goeth, because the darkness hath blinded his eyes." (I John 2:9,11)

CHAPTER 24

Don't Shoot — I'm Already Wounded

By the early 1980's, we could no longer keep our doors open. The financial recession hit our area especially hard, and that with the continuing Church boycott brought us down. We forgave the customers who left town to look for work, leaving us with unpaid bills and uncollected checks. They were having a hard time too, and even if they had all paid up it would not have saved us. Our inventory was sadly depleted, and our accounts payable nullified our checkbook. We were insolvent.

We rejected the recommendation that we should file bankruptcy and get debt-free the American way.

Instead, we moved the remaining contents of our once well-stocked 2,800 square foot store into our single-car garage and tried to "hang on" until better times.

What we hadn't counted on was the unmerciful harassment by hard-nosed credit managers, the insulting and dehumanizing collection agencies, the hired-for-a-percentage attorneys. There is an uncanny sense within the "system" when someone's back is against the wall; they move in for the kill. Our big buying days were over; there was no more fawning solicitation of our purchasing power. The JEU companies and publishers of yesterday turned into avid hunters of today.

I had previously been in the business world for over 30 years. At one time I owed over ten times what I now owed, but I received more understanding and better treatment from pagans than I was now getting from those who profess to believe in the King of Love. The insulting letters, the incriminating phone calls were driving my once loving and giving wife to the funny farm. Not inured to the insults and unmerciful abuse, she began falling apart, her nerves ripped to shreds. All she could do was cry, and cry she did. Watching the object of your love being hurt and destroyed by "Christians" sets a man into a frame of mind he never knew he was capable of.

I am not talking about large amounts. The amount we owed to any one company was not large. We were nailed to the wall for nickels and dimes compared to the thousands upon thousands of dollars we had given each company for merchandise in years past. For example, one of the biggest names in the "Christian jewelry" business, one who himself admits he became a millionaire selling jewelry to Christians, turned us over to collection for a debt of $21.15! A prominent California Jesus-junk dealer took us to small claims court to collect $60.27 **for interest only!** We had paid the bill, but he wanted the interest badly enough to go to court.

One of the biggest "Christian" book distributors on the West Coast put a lien on our home to collect $44.67 **for interest only** on a once past-due invoice. Another big-name "Christian" publisher hired an attorney to sue us for not being able to pay an outstanding bill of $108.44. Of course, the summons read $368.30 — $259.86 was added for interest! Please note the favorable and "inside" interest rates that these JEU companies charge their brethren — you pay interest on the interest on top of the interest. It is strange to note that the secular companies that we owed money to did not ever harass us, nor did they ever charge us interest.

These are only a few examples of uncaring, deliberately merciless dealings that left us with a psychological wound that I doubt will ever be healed. "Christian" businessmen had a way of punishing those who fall from their favor that is unknown even among the heathen.

People wonder why we now run away from those who announce themselves to us as "Christian." We feel we need to wait until we see the evidence.

CHAPTER 25

Phone Call from Heaven

When we closed the doors on our business, we did not have the phone disconnected. We were going to try to carry on at home, and we hoped that some of the countless numbers of customers that we prayed for, counseled, or helped in some way would order something from us to keep us alive. A few did, but so many followed the instructions of their spiritual leaders to boycott us that they drove 30-some miles to the next Christian bookstore — in spite of our 20% discount on all purchases. How is it that a Christian can go to so much trouble, expense, and lost time just to "boycott" another Christian? Regardless of anyone's opinion, it seemed to be poor stewardship of their money!

Our hearts were crushed over our "failure." Further, our pockets were very much "to let," as the saying goes. So the constant ringing of the phone with inhuman collection agencies, threatening attorneys, and irate credit managers whose chief purpose in life seemed to be to harass us day and night really put us in despair.

One morning, the phone rang as usual right at 8 o'clock, and the caller wanted to know why we had not paid their bill. It was exactly $15.90. I again painfully explained our situation and our inability to pay anything or anybody at this time. The caller wanted to know my full name. I knew what that meant; they were preparing legal papers to serve me. Then the lady asked for my wife's name. I gave it to her—after all, I thought, why should she miss out on all these nifty experiences in the JEU business. Then the caller's next statement almost knocked me off my chair.

"As soon as I hang up, we are going to bring you and your wife's name before the Lord. We would like to pray for both of you. Is that all right?"

I was so choked up, I could scarcely speak. Of all the countless people we had always prayed for, only a handful had even suggested that they would or even wanted to pray for us. Yet here was a perfect stranger calling from another state saying they were going to pray in our behalf! After all the other calloused calls, I could not believe this one. I was so taken aback that all I could manage was a tearful "thank you."

A few days later, I got my usual monthly statement from this very publisher. It showed my balance as usual. But across the paper was written, "Paid in Full." They had written off our bill! But that's not all. Enclosed in the same envelope was a cashier's check for over a hundred dollars, plus over $20.00 in cash! Now I really couldn't believe it. They not only absorbed my debt, they multiplied that amount several times and sent it to me in cash!

Miracles do still happen, even in these "latter days." May God richly bless those lovely saints!

The perplexing paradox of this unexpected blessing is that we had not done that much business with this particular publisher. It was a very small company, and our account with them was tiny compared to the tens of thousands of dollars' business we had given to others. But, thank God, there are still genuine Christian people in the world. That knowledge was about all that kept us sane throughout the rest of that day.

The phone rang again. I just happened to be looking at a large publisher's catalog, admiring a picture of their new multi-million-dollar facility, and the caller happened to be them. The voice on the other end of the line was cold and stern. If we did not pay our past-due bill **today** he was going to notify the IRS. The IRS? What does the Internal Revenue Service have to do with my bill with this JEU company? Unless he wanted their goon-squad; they are supposed to be able to squeeze money from poor unfortunate souls even when there is none to squeeze.

Then there was a knock on the door. It was the sheriff serving papers drawn up by a "Bible-belt" JEU publisher suing us for $178.56. What had happened to 1st Corinthians, where Paul clearly states that Christians are not to sue one another? We are instructed to accept a wrong and even be defrauded if need be, rather than go to law. Now, of course, business argues that business is business, and you can't run a business on air, or even hopes and dreams. But this business had already made a huge profit from us; would it really have cost them anything to wait a while for the remainder of our money? Indeed, if the small publisher could forgive a debt, could not also a super large one?

Others of these publishers turned us over to collection agencies, attorneys, or sued for the **interest** due after we had paid the principal of the debt. Does no one take into account the Word of God that says, " . . . thou shalt not be to him as an usurer, neither shalt thou lay upon him usury." (Ex. 22:25). "Thou shalt not lend upon usury to thy brother . . . " (Deut. 23:19). Granted we are living in difficult financial times; but God's word is full of assurances that He is able to overcome and bless even in difficult times. His promise is, "Charge no interest, so that the Lord your God may bless you in all your enterprises." It would seem that businesses should be able to trust God as well as individuals — especially Christian businesses? Perhaps the reason they need the money so badly they must lift their hand against their brother is because they do not have God's blessing . . . and they do not have God's blessing because they lift their hands against brethren. Who will deliver us from this vicious circle?

As for me and my house, we have to trust the Lord in spite of the bad examples of the twentieth-century JEU business. We love and pray for those blessed ones who forgave our debts and even helped us in our distress. We pray, too, for those who despitefully used us, that they yet become Christians and experience God's grace, so they may show grace to others!

CHAPTER 26

Business . . . or Ministry?

Like the chicken and the egg, it is hard to tell which comes first. In reflecting on my failed business . . . or was it my ministry? . . . I've almost concluded that the place to begin is to decide if we do, indeed, have a chicken. We call them "Christian" bookstores, but are they Christian or merely "religious" bookstores? There **is** a difference.

A bonafide Christian bookstore, I should think, would be expected to carry only things pertaining to the Christian faith. There are hundreds of religions in the world, but only one Christian faith. The Scriptures are rather dogmatic about mixing the Christian faith with other religions. If we called our store a religious store, we would be free to carry anything and every-

This is a picture of me inside our "garage" ministry. I still teach and I still preach and we still pray for and with people. Counseling takes a lot of my time; people still hurt and they still need honest answers to honest questions. But the rent is due, Lord; can You provide just one more time?

thing pertaining to any kind of religion. But if we call it a Christian store, we are automatically restricted to what the Scriptures call Christian. The Scriptures are the only record we have of Christ, and He was careful to honor only "what was written."

Our mistake appears to be that we thought of our store as a Christian bookstore and we wished to honor, as much as possible, only what was written. I say "as much as possible" because it was not possible to read every page of every book before we put it in the store. But if we knew something was erroneous, that is, did not reflect Scriptural truth, we returned it or refused to carry it. This practice, of all things, branded us as "peculiar" in the Christian (so-called) community.

The Christian bookstore is in an impossible situation. It is between a rock and a hard place. On one side is the publisher who wants to push "what sells," regardless of how trashy or unscriptural or antichrist it is, and on the other side is the religious public who wants to buy the trash.

Personally, I think items like votive candles and rosary beads are artifacts borrowed from pagan religions and have no place in the Christian faith. The same holds for statues or images. I simply could not feel right about selling statues of St. Christopher for people to put on their dashboards for "protection."

Putting superstitious faith into an artifact of wood or metal or stone is expressly forbidden by Scripture, as are repetitious prayers learned by rote and many other practices that go with these "religious" artifacts. This problem may not arise in larger cities where there is enough business to support both religious bookstores and Christian bookstores, but it became an issue in our small suburb. We were "blacklisted" by group after group because we did not bow to their Baals.

Even in the larger cities, where Christian bookstores have a larger card and gift department than book department, we see a heavy catering to "what sells." And what sells seems to be something short of what's truly Christian. The stores have to stay in business, and apparently to stay in business you have to cater to the public taste.

The problem moves, then, to the people who buy. Why do they wish to buy untrue books, sensational thrillers that don't reflect truth? Again, the people are not being taught what truth is, and how to tell truth from falsehood. So the Church structure and practice is faulty. Who began it? Who is really to blame? The chicken or the egg?

It appears that the publishers, the bookstores, and even the churches have all been carried away with one thing: profit. An exclusively Christian bookstore could not stay in business for 30 days; there are not enough laity around who are interested in truth to support them.

If a bookstore owner is honest, he will admit that he could not survive on selling only "orthodox" material. He would confess that his business depends on his selection of non-Christian (religious) books and trinkets. These religious items are what keeps his doors open.

I am about as angry at the "Christian" booksellers as I can be — I would like to blame them for the way things are today. Yet Jeremiah blamed the people themselves. They supported the false prophets by listening to them. Perhaps the only way out is for people to rise up in rebellion against "big business" and demand the old way of truth. Is it possible? It doesn't seem so . . . but it has happened before a few times in history.

Sometimes one has to fail in order to succeed. If we had continued to be a money-making "ministry," as we were at first, we would no doubt wrongly believe that God was blessing us. We had to fail in our "ministry" to realize that bookstores like ours, even though we tried to keep our inventory "clean," was illegal in the eyes of God. The whole JEU SELLS syndrome has to be thrown out of the temple of God. Thank you, Lord, for our failure, for in it we found a true victory.

This building was once our Christian bookstore. The religious community boycotted us until we were forced to close it down. It is now a Video store that sells and rents "adult" movies. The religious community has no objection.

CHAPTER 27

Tribulation and Revelation

Seven years ago, the first hot-air balloons "for JEU" floated skyward announcing the grand opening of our Christian bookstore. We had prepared for months, putting our best efforts into a well-decorated and well-stocked store. With the right music playing in the background, we opened the store and celebrated. There were handshakes, hugs, smiles, and rejoicing.

Now, seven years later, financially broke (but somewhat wiser), I reflect on those seven years and I realize they are neatly divided into two periods of 3 1/2 years each — just like the legendary dispensational tradition. We had 3 1/2 years of peace and prosperity, and 3 1/2 years of hellish persecution.

We have already had our great tribulation!

Although it took longer than seven calendar years, I see a parallel in our whole Christian lives. I well remember those early Christian experiences. The Sunday services were wonderful times of fellowship and rejoicing. We had the appropriate music in the background, and we circulated among our fellow believers with handshakes, smiles, and Jesus hugs. "Praise the Lord" was the password into all things wonderful for us newborn King's Kids. Health and wealth were ours for the asking. We were hilarious over our joyful "secrets," so we shouted, praised, danced, and sang. Did we not have all this and heaven too? Away with gloom and doom.

Our world was neatly marked out for us. It was sharply divided between "us and them." We were better, smarter, holy and saved. They were lower, stupid, ungodly, and hellbound. Shooting stars and the party spirit were for us. Tribulation and affliction were only for pagans, or "weak in the faith" — and, perhaps, for those far-off and unlucky Christians behind the Iron Curtain. We managed not to think about them too much; God had obviously blessed America with affluence and freedom of religion, and it was up to us to redound to God's glory by making the most of it. If we lined our pockets with money, well, that also was to the glory of God and furnished the proof of our selfish theology.

Little did I know, in those days, that in the fellowship of the saints, when one suffers, we all suffer. The true Church of Jesus Christ has **always** suffered, whenever or wherever on our planet, including our own dear USA. If the Church in America today seems to be escaping its normal dose of persecution, it is because it has compromised to a great extent with the philosophies of the world it lives in.

Everybody loves the heal-me-bless-me-get-me-rich-quick gospel. Nobody persecutes that! Indeed, they join it. Thus the modern "church" in America is filled with people whose hearts have never undergone change. They are in it for what it offers them.

Somewhere along the way, in our happy flight from reality, we were slowly but steadily apprehended by Truth. The Holy and Sovereign God of the Bible emerged from its pages to change us. We began to care about Truth. We began to talk about it. We began to seek it in the books we read, comparing them with God's Word, and rejecting the ones that did not pass the test. We began to stand with Jeremiah, declaring that God's Word was the only hammer that could break the rock in pieces (Jer. 23:29). We took note of Jesus' instruction to "take heed what ye hear" (Mark 4:24). We began to follow John's advice and put everything to the test (I John 4:1). With the help of a teacher, whom we have always felt was sent of God, we began to love and explore God's Word. And the more we loved it, the more sharply we felt the rocky resistance of opposition in the world . . . and not only in the world but in the Church infiltrated by the world.

Jesus said, "In the world ye **shall** have tribulation" (John 16:33). He did not say this because He was a sadist, but because He was a realist. The spirit of God has always been the mortal enemy of the spirit that is in the world; the two can never reconcile.

God allows this condition to exist, while this world lasts, for a good reason. Without tribulation, our yearnings would be identical with Mrs. Lots'. Our hearts would stay behind in Sodom, where they would eventually die, instead of ascending to heaven with our Great Treasure.

Normal human beings avoid suffering of any kind if they can. We postpone the dentist's chair to the last possible moment. His "open wide" means something unpleasant to us, and so we go along chewing on the other side of our mouth - - the side that is not yet sore. But when the condition worsens, when we are tormented beyond endurance, then our opinion about the dentist takes a turnabout. Sometimes we are so anxious to get there we can hardly wait! We explode when we find he has a waiting list! Go ahead and drill, Mr. Dentist, and be quick about it. Do what you have to, but relieve me of this pain! Suddenly our enemy the dentist has become our dearest friend, our saviour. What changed our minds? Simple. Tribulation! Without pain, we would still be in the candy store pacifying our rotting sweet tooth.

Tribulation, the tool of the enemy, becomes an instrument of God. He is not the author of tribulation, He has declared that in His word, but He uses it, as He uses all things, to bring eventual good into the lives of His people. Everything, even tribulation, must bow to the sovereignty of God — for He has declared that all things will be turned into eventual good (Rom. 8:28).

The harm done by the "health and wealth" religions will probably not be fully known until revealed at the Last Day. The idea of "King's kids" who deserve all the best — the best car, the best job, the best house, the best billing on the popularity list — has the effect of setting our hearts in the wrong place. We would stay in the candy store; we would stay in Sodom. We have it all right here, so why do we need heaven? Yet, woe to him who withholds the Truth from the ears of the unsaved and feeds them a candy-coated lie instead (Isa. 56:10-11; Ezek. 33:2-6; Acts 10:42). The end thereof is destruction, rottenness all through.

Jesus said we would be hated (Matt. 10:22), excluded, insulted, and denounced (Luke 6:22), slandered and persecuted, even dragged into court (Luke 21:12). Right here, in modern times, in the USA, I was denounced from pulpits as "dangerous," boycotted, slandered, sued, taken to court, and forced out of business. Not by the world, **but by "Christians!"** By "King's kids" who cared not for Truth and even hated it.

Truth is an expensive commodity. Who knows its real value? Jesus stood alone, deserted even by friends, when He stood for Truth. His costly Gospel is still excluded and persecuted. Mind you, in our bookstore, I was not introducing some new philosophy I had thought of myself. I tried to promote books that have always been considered pillars of the faith once delivered to the saints, written by men of the Reformation who have always been considered the foundation of the Church. For this, I was denounced.

We were persecuted for refusing to stock certain books. The memory of one such book still makes the hairs prickle on the back of my neck, so false was it. It bears an alarming parallel to the preposterous lies of Joseph Smith, complete with heavenly visitations of false doctrines "right from the angels." We lost one segment of customers because of our stand on this blatantly false book.

In our town, the opposition came chiefly from the candy-coated "gospel" enthusiasts. The second wave came from the new, independent clericalism that says "I am your chief, your prophet — all your allegiance (and incidentally your money) belongs to **me.** I have a new revelation, listen only to me . . ." And sealing our doom was the apathy (and even sometimes opposition) of the mainstream churches who still claim the names begun in the Reformation. Deceivers who should be driven from the Church by the sword of Truth prevailed over us, and we found no one to stand with us.

We lost more than our store. We lost years of our lives. Our home is still in jeopardy. Our future looks grim, for at our age it is very difficult to get a job or a fresh start.

One thing this experience has done for us: we have nothing left to lose. We are determined to continue to defend the Gospel of Jesus Christ. If we can't preach Truth from a store, then we'll preach it from our garage. If they take away our garage, we'll preach it from a street corner. If they take away our street corner, we'll publish it and let that be our voice. If we die for that, so be it. Heaven looks good to us now.